BUDDHISM AND ETHNIC CONFLICT IN SRI LANKA

SUNY series in Religious Studies
Harold Coward, editor

BUDDHISM AND ETHNIC CONFLICT IN SRI LANKA

Patrick Grant

SUNY
PRESS

Published by State University of New York Press, Albany

Printed in the United States of America

For information, contact State University of New York Press, Albany, NY
www.sunypress.edu

Production by Ryan Morris
Marketing by Michael Campochiaro

Library of Congress Cataloging-in-Publication Data

Grant, Patrick, 1941–
    Buddhism and ethnic conflict in Sri Lanka / Patrick Grant.
        p. cm. — (SUNY series in religious studies)
    Includes bibliographical references and index.
    ISBN 978-0-7914-9353-3 (hardcover : alk. paper)
    ISBN 978-0-7914-9354-0 (pbk. : alk. paper)   1.Buddhist renewal—
Sri Lanka.   2. Nationalism—Religious aspects—Buddhism.   3. Ethnic conflict—
Sri Lanka.   I. Title.
    BQ374.G73 2009
    294.3095493—dc22
                                                                                2008017375
                            10 9 8 7 6 5 4 3 2 1

For
Henry Summerfield

And we, alone again under an oblivious sky, were quick to learn how our best construals of divinity, our *Do unto*, *Love*, *Don't kill*, could be easily garbled to canticles of vengeance and battle-prayers.

C. K. Williams, War

CONTENTS

PREFACE

The seeds of this study were sown in 1960 when I entered Queen's University in Belfast, Northern Ireland, as an undergraduate. At that time, Gamini Salgado was a lecturer in English, specializing in Renaissance drama. He was a favorite among students—mildly bohemian, captivating, eloquent. His remarkable lectures were, somehow, the product of a natural flamboyant energy combined with abrasive critical intelligence. Also, Gamini was from Ceylon.

In Northern Ireland during the early to mid-1960s, civil unrest was gathering a momentum that would soon erupt into the violent conflict that was to last for more than thirty years. By the end of the decade, long-standing antagonisms between the Unionist ("Protestant") majority and Nationalist ("Catholic") minority had taken a catastrophically virulent turn, and Northern Ireland thereafter rapidly found its way to becoming one of the world's most widely publicized ethnic conflict zones.

Even before the violence of the late 1960s, the religious divide in Northern Ireland was taboo for lecturers at Queen's, who were required not to address the politico-religious debate in their teaching. But, for personal reasons, I had a special interest in connections between religion and literature, and soon developed an extracurricular conversation with Gamini about Ceylon, and how Buddhism played into the political situation there. This was my first introduction to both Buddhism and to Sri Lanka (as Ceylon has been called since 1972).

Gamini eventually left Queen's to take a post at the University of Sussex where, by coincidence, I went to read for a D.Phil. And so the conversation continued (including, this time, lessons in Sri Lankan cooking). My interest in Buddhism developed from these beginnings, and was influenced from the start by what I saw as an affinity between modern Sri Lanka and modern Northern Ireland.

After I left Sussex, my academic career was taken up for many years with the writing of a series of books, mostly about religion (Christianity, in particular), literature, and politics. Then, in the late 1990s, I returned to the source, as it were, and eventually published two books about religion and violent ethnic conflict in modern Northern Ireland. As I was working on these books, I found myself increasingly preoccupied by the fact that similarly structured ethnonationalist conflicts had sprung up across the world in the second half of the twentieth century (Bosnia, Lebanon, Sudan, Rwanda, among others—including, more recently, Iraq). And so I thought I could best learn more about this widespread phenomenon by turning to my interest in Buddhism (which had continued to develop over the years) and to the political problems of Sri Lanka, to which I had been introduced a long time previously.

These remarks can help to clarify the approach I am taking in the present study. That is, I hope to make some central aspects of the Sri Lankan conflict accessible, especially to Western readers, and to that end I provide an introductory account of the main teachings of Theravada Buddhism. I also make suggestions about the literary dynamics of the Buddha's Discourses, which I believe are important for understanding the Buddha's teaching practice and how it informs, or fails to inform, modern interpreters. I then focus on three influential Sinhala Buddhist writers whose works are in large part translated into English, and whose agenda is the revival of what they take to be a pure Buddhism, interpreted in the context of Sri Lanka's political independence from Britain. These writers do not represent the full range of Sri Lankan opinion about the independence movement and the ensuing ethnonationalist conflict. Rather, they show the workings of a process I describe as "regressive inversion," which offers some explanation of the means by which religion can be dangerously annexed to ethnonationalist interests, not just in Sri Lanka, but elsewhere.

During the 1970s, I had come across the idea of "moral inversion" in the writings of Michael Polanyi, who explains modern secular nihilism as a violent recoil of idealism upon the educational and social institutions that gave shape to that same idealism in the first place. The irony by which a liberating discourse might set loose forces that end up destroying liberty I found highly interesting, even though such a process does not quite describe the phenomena of ethnoreligious conflict. And so I have proposed the term "regressive inversion" to describe what happens when a universally liberating religious vision is re-deployed to supercharge the passions associated with loyalty to a group. This process is *regressive* insofar as it reaffirms an exclusionary identity (the very thing that the universal religious vision was designed to transcend). Also, it entails an *inversion* of value insofar as it draws power from the languages of transcendence, informed as these are by aspirations to an absolute liberation.

In part I of the following study, I discuss some implications of regressive inversion for Buddhism, and how insightfully the Buddha deals with relationships between his own liberating vision and the Vedic tradition from which it emerged and which placed a heavy emphasis on caste and social distinctions.

As history shows, the idea that a person can be spiritually liberated regardless of kin, class, cult, or status was far from self-evident and had to be discovered. The period when this kind of discovery was first making itself felt among many of the world's major religions is sometimes known as the Axial Age, extending roughly from 900 to 200 B.C.E. Central to Axial Age thinking is the claim that believers are defined by their individual adherence to a transcendent principle or reality. By comparison with the integrity of that interior observance and the compassion and selflessness that flow from it, external factors such as cult practice, social or family obligation, and the like were held to be insignificant.

Buddhism provides an especially good example of this kind of Axial Age universalism. Basically, Buddhist meditation and instruction are concerned to free people from attachments, because ties that bind cause only suffering. Consequently, liberation entails the relinquishment of every desire and selfish concern; also, it requires no ritual appeasements or invocations, and does not depend on caste or other forms of group allegiance.

In a pure form, the Buddha's teachings on such matters are austere and demanding and Buddhist monks (*bhikkhus*) are, in a sense, specialists who are able to devote sufficient time to the discipline of meditation and to exemplifying nonattachment in their daily lives. By their presence and example, the *bhikkhus* ensure that laypeople are kept mindful of Buddhism's high ideals, and, in return, the *bhikkhus* receive material support from the laity.

Nonetheless, although the idea of an individually achieved liberation remains central to Buddhism, it is also the case that our basic nurture as human beings entails a variety of attachments and dependencies. Only someone who has been nurtured within a group and who is able to feel sustained by a sense of belonging can emerge into a healthy adulthood with sufficient independence to grasp the moral force of the key Axial Age ideas in the first place. Even people who commit themselves wholeheartedly to a higher principle of nonattachment are not likely to remain indifferent to their families and to the cultures in which they grew up and to which they owe some degree of loyalty based on deeply enculturated feeling-structures. The recommended transcendence of attachments therefore needs to be managed discerningly in relation to our actual, humanizing relationships with those who are close to us and who have provided for us. On the one hand, excessive idealism, and, on the other, mere submergence of one's identity within a group are therefore best avoided. Yet these alternatives are not mutually exclusive and can easily become confused. The process I describe as regressive inversion offers a telling example of such confusion, which occurs when aspirations to a universal ideal are deployed to intensify the kind of group solidarity that the ideal itself requires us to transcend.

For instance, imagine a neighbor harming your cat or dog (or, let us not think about it, your child). You call the police so that the higher principles enshrined in law can adjudicate the case. Understandably, your recourse to the law might not assuage the anger and hostility you feel toward your neighbor; nonetheless, you contain yourself out of respect for the principles informing the legal process. But should the law then fail to provide a satisfactory resolution, you might well find yourself even more angry, perhaps inclined to take matters into your own hands. Your actions then are fired by a conviction that justice must be done, and in the name of a thwarted ideal you are, as it were, implacably angry rather than just passionately so. The term "regressive inversion" is shorthand for this perplexing but dangerous state of mind, the unintended offshoot of an idealism that would liberate us from the very violence that, in certain circumstances, it endows with a boundless intensity.

My argument in part I suggests that Buddhism is a great religion not least because of the manner in which it deals with the dangers of regressive inversion. Although meditation is central to Buddhist practice, the Buddha also teaches discursively, by way of verbal communication. And, as the Pali Canon (the body of texts with which I am most concerned) shows, the Buddha deals repeatedly with a wide range of people whose worldly attachments and loyalties are impediments to the universal truth that he proclaims. Throughout his discourses, the Buddha repeatedly confronts the recalcitrance of a wide range of interlocutors, using various rhetorical strategies to wean them away from attachments and habits of mind that impede their understanding of his core message. For the most part, these attachments are to the rituals, myths, and philosophy of Vedic tradition; indeed, much of the language in which the Buddha himself proclaimed his teaching was also that of the Vedas. The Buddha's new vision therefore remains embedded in older practices that enable its expression. Yet the Discourses also show the Buddha's skill in assessing how people are negatively affected by encultured feeling-structures that compromise their ability to interpret his main teaching about liberation, and he adjusts his style of conversation accordingly.

In chapter 1, I describe these concerns by distinguishing between a predominantly "conjunctive" (Vedic) and a predominantly "disjunctive" (Buddhist) use of language. In practice, these different emphases cannot be fully separated, and, short of *nibbana* (a "blowing out" of all the traces of discourse and attachment), we need to preserve a vigilant sense of how they can remain fruitfully in dialogue. In chapter 2, I am especially concerned with how this dialogue is conducted within the Buddha's Discourses: as I have mentioned, the Buddha offers a remarkable range of strategies to engage his interlocutors, taking into account their passionate ("conjunctive") involvements, and adjusting his austere, universal ("disjunctive") message accordingly, to prevent the dangerous confusions that might arise from a misunderstanding of his instructions about radical nonattachment.

One main problem in modern ethnic conflict zones involving religion is that such dangerous confusions do in fact prevail, as passionately felt loyalties are infused with an absolute, religious significance. The boundless aspirations inspired by a transcendent, disjunctive religious vision are then annexed to the exclusionist, conjunctive identity that the religion itself requires us to transcend. As we shall see in part II, modern Sri Lanka provides a compelling and disturbing example of this process.

Part II deals with Sri Lanka, focusing on three influential Sinhala Buddhists who wrote immediately before, during, and after the period of Sri Lanka's independence from Britain in 1948. As part of the independence struggle, all three advocate the revival of what they take to be a pure Buddhism, but in so doing they also exemplify the seductions and dangers of regressive inversion.

To show how modern Sri Lankan Buddhists were, for historical reasons, often predisposed to interpret the Pali Canon in support of a Sinhala national identity, I begin part II with an account of the ancient Sri Lankan chronicle tradition. The *Mahavamsa*, written in the sixth century (C.E.) was composed by *bhikkhus* to address and consolidate relationships between the monarchy and the Buddhist monastic community (*Sangha*). The *Mahavamsa* offers a legendary account of the origins of Sinhala civilization, and provides a historical chronicle of its monarchs and their support for Buddhism, as well as their armed resistance to non-Buddhist usurpers. Although the *Mahavamsa* does not have a modern understanding of national or ethnic identity, it stresses that Sri Lanka's legitimate rulers have been Sinhala Buddhists, and that their authority is confirmed by the Buddha himself (who is said to have visited Sri Lanka on three occasions, flying through the air to get there).

Modern Buddhist revivalists have often looked especially to the *Mahavamsa* to confirm their arguments in support of a Sinhala Buddhist national culture. In doing so, they have frequently imposed on the *Mahavamsa* modern theories about race (derived from Western sources) and about national identity. The result is a racialized and nationalist rereading of the chronicle, which had already insisted on a Sinhala Buddhist exceptionalism in contradiction to what (as we now see) the Pali Canon teaches. Chapter 3, on the *Mahavamsa*, therefore provides a bridge between the opening discussion of the Buddha's Discourses and the writings of the modern revivalists whom I discuss subsequently.

The three figures on whom I concentrate in chapters 4 to 6 are Anagarika Dharmapala (1864–1933), Walpola Rahula (1907–1997), and J. R. Jayewardene (1906–1996). All three were highly influential in shaping an independent postcolonial Sri Lanka, but in each, also, regressive inversion gives rise to contradictions that become evident when their writings are examined in relation to what we have learned about the Buddha's actual teaching in the Pali Canon.

A summary of certain key contradictions that (as I will argue in detail) opened the way to regressive inversion in the writings and policies of these three figures runs, briefly, as follows. Dharmapala's optimistic trust in modern science to establish a golden age Sinhala Buddhist utopia causes him to misestimate the dangers of an exclusionism that he also promotes, and which becomes an impediment to the very progress he desires. Rahula's scholarly appreciation of Buddhist nonviolence stands uncomfortably opposed to his espousals of militarism in support of Sinhala Buddhist hegemony, and three considerations help to explain how this is so: first, Rahula's appeal to a principle of relativity in interpreting the Buddha's teachings; second, his rereading of the *Mahavamsa*; third, his lack of sympathy for how traditional Buddhist practices mediate the Buddha's teachings in an imperfect world. Jayewardene strongly opposed the kind of *bhikkhu* activism advocated by Rahula, and insisted that the monks stay out of politics. But Jayewardene also promoted a Sinhala Buddhist cultural nationalism, handsomely supported by state funds. Although he supplies careful arguments to justify his policies, his intellectual sophistication was overwhelmed by the passionate intensity of the conflict to which, tragically, his own cultural agenda contributed. In the analysis of the writings of these figures, my central claim is that in all of them we see the liberating vision of a great religion redeployed in unfortunate ways to confirm and intensify prejudices that the religion itself expressly repudiates.

Throughout this study, I concentrate on language and its interpretation, but I do so not without realizing that there is a great deal more to the religious and political issues I discuss than language alone. Nonetheless, words remain our special privilege and liability. We are civilized because we have language, but we are dangerous because we can effectively plan the destruction of what we have built. Yes, we are more complex than the languages we speak, but we surrender at our peril the vigilance required to allow our languages to build for us rather than destroy.

I remain immensely indebted to Gamini Salgado, who died in 1985, and without whom I would not have found my way to writing this book. I would like also to thank Radhika Desai for getting me involved in 2003; David Little and Jonathan Spencer for valuable advice about Sri Lanka; Harold Coward for his much appreciated expertise, especially in the Hindu traditions (and for crucially important encouragement otherwise); Martin Adam for his expertise in Buddhism; Laurence Lerner and Henry Summerfield for, as ever, making helpful suggestions and wise critical observations. Sue Mitchell prepared the typescript, and, as so frequently in the past, she is the mainstay without whom I certainly would not have made landfall.

A version of chapter 5 was published as "Imagining Buddhism in Sri Lanka: Walpola Rahula and Gamini Salgado," *Studies in Religion/Sciences Religieuses* 33/3–4 (2004): 415–427.

PART I

READING BUDDHISM

CHAPTER 1

VEDIC TRADITION
AND THE BUDDHA

HOW TO SAY THE UNSAYABLE

In this chapter I will describe how Buddhism is nourished by the ancient Vedic religious traditions from which it also stands separate. To express its distinctive position, Buddhism emphasizes a use of language that I will describe (following Thomas M. Greene) as "disjunctive," in contrast to a richly "conjunctive" discourse of the Vedas, expressing how the world is suffused with a divine significance that can be directed and manipulated by sacrifice and other rituals.

Despite the Buddha's departure from tradition, the Pali Canon (the foundational texts of Theravada Buddhism, with which I am mostly concerned) remains infused by its Vedic antecedents. This is so not least because disjunctive and conjunctive uses of language are not in fact separable, even though they are theorectically distinct. This point remains central to my larger argument because it enables us to see how Buddhist discourse is engaged from the start in a complex dialogue. As the Buddha knew—and as I will show in some detail in chapter 2—teaching through dialogue enables nuanced judgments about how people's religious aspirations relate to their historical circumstances, personal aptitudes, prejudices, and passionate loyalties. In turn, such judgments do much to prevent the misappropriation of the Buddha's teaching by special interests driven by prejudice, lack of understanding, or wrongheaded enthusiasm. To explore these claims in more detail, let us begin by considering some key Buddhist ideas about language.

DIALOGUE AND THE LIMITS OF LANGUAGE

Buddhism sets us on the way to liberation, yet Buddhism requires also a radical distrust of every attempt to describe what liberation is. This distrust is based on the fact that reality is more complex than language. To be liberated is to extinguish every trace of individual separateness and self-centered desire; these are delusions, transient determinations of a wholly unconditioned reality. But language is itself transient and fragmented and is encompassed by the unconditioned, which it cannot therefore be expected to describe.

Even in everyday usage, language bears an uncertain relationship to its objects. Suppose I change the head of my axe; would I say I have the same axe, or a different one? (What if I then change the handle?) And if I take my bicycle to pieces, at what point does it cease to be a bicycle? The Buddhist monk Nagasena imagined a chariot when he used a version of this argument to show King Milinda[1] how readily words can induce in us a false sense of permanence and certainty.

The idea that ultimate reality is mysterious beyond description is itself not uncommon among the world's spiritual writers. Thus, the Christian philosopher-theologian Nicholas of Cusa (1401–1464) declares of God that if anyone should say, "Thou wert called by this name or that, by the very fact that he named it, I should know that it was not Thy name."[2] In spirit, this is not far removed from Lao-Tsu's opening verse in the *Tao Te Ching*, compiled perhaps in the fourth century B.C.E.: "The way that can be spoken of / Is not the constant way."[3] That is, as soon as we name the Tao, it is not the Tao that we name.

Although it is not difficult to find examples of this kind, it is the case also that Buddhism is the first major philosophical or religious movement[4] to thematize the discontinuity between language and reality, and to establish a critical approach to semiotics as a principal teaching. Typically, Buddhism stresses how an uncritical dependency on language keeps us agitated and dissatisfied; consequently, liberating ourselves from the nets of our own anxieties and desires will require (at least) a scrupulously discerning attitude to words and how we use them.

When the Sakyan Prince, Siddhattha Gotama,[5] became enlightened as a Buddha, he decided at first not to impart his newfound knowledge to others. After all, how could he explain enlightenment without giving people the wrong idea? Language being what it is, wouldn't any idea be the wrong idea? The God Brahma is said to have convinced the enlightened Gotama to change his mind, and the Buddha's teachings subsequently found expression in a body of writing of immense variety and complexity. Nonetheless, throughout the Discourses of the Pali Canon, the Buddha resolutely pulls away every conceptual support to which his interlocutors might cling for solace in a world where—as the Buddha insists—all things are impermanent and marked by suffering. Dogma, rituals, imaginings, hopes, fears, traditions, friendships, families, social institutions—these offer only a false security, temporarily shoring up our fragile ego against the ceaseless change that is basic to existence itself.

What then are we to learn from the voluminous Buddhist scriptures? On the face of it, they are full of prescriptions, rules, classifications, itemized codes of behavior, and complex analyses. Clearly, much energy is invested here in language, even as the deceptiveness of language is everywhere held to be a main impediment to spiritual progress.

One way to approach this question is to notice that the Buddha's teaching is in large part dialogical. That is, he deals with his interlocutors in the manner made famous at a later date in Western philosophy by Socrates, though one main difference is that Socrates (according to Plato) uses dialogue to awaken his interlocutors to the metaphysical reality of ideas, whereas the Buddha wants to do the opposite. That is, the Buddha wants people to know that ideas are another form of attachment, a deflection from the reality in which every distinction—including even consciousness—is relinquished, burnt-out entirely, and consumed without trace. This reality beyond distinction is liberation, *nibbana*, about which, of course, nothing substantive can be said.

Meditation is the central practice by which Buddhists learn to put aside distractions, opening themselves to the unconditioned. But in the realm of discourse, with which I am mainly concerned and which aims to impart knowledge to others, dialogue becomes an effective way to lead people toward an intuition of the unrepresentable truth about *nibbana*. This is so because insight can occur in the interstices of the dialogical exchange—on the undecided ground, as it were, between conflicting points of view. Insight is therefore provoked by dialogue rather than produced by it through direct instruction or demonstration. Encouraging someone by such means to let go of an unhelpful, ingrained opinion or attachment requires a skillful deployment of argument and counter-argument aimed at bringing the interlocutor to a point where the penny drops and some fresh insight springs up to disclose the limitations and folly of an ingrained prejudice or habit of mind. It is as if the interlocutor discovers this new perspective for him or her self, and to enable such a result, the Buddha recommends the deployment of "skillful action" (*kusala-kamma*), taking into account character, circumstance, the complexity of the opinion to be debated, and so on. The aim is for some degree of awakening to occur, though the dialogue in itself cannot guarantee to produce it. And if awakening does occur, the dialogue all at once can seem redundant, somehow beside the point, as words once again are consumed by the truth to which they refer but do not encompass.

As an assessor of the Buddha's rhetorical strategies and psychological insights, a reader of the Discourses is also engaged in the dialogical process. Sometimes, indeed, the reader might prove a better understander of the Buddha's message than the person to whom the Buddha is speaking within the text, and complexities attendant upon characterization and manipulation of viewpoint throughout the Discourses call for a nuanced and tactful reader-response. Certainly, compassionate discernment remains as significant for Buddhism as are the doctrinal formulations frequently described as Buddhism's "core" teachings. Although doctrines such as the Four Noble Truths and the Noble Eightfold Path certainly are important, they are also abstract and prescriptive. By contrast, people's actual experience is typically complex, made up of passionate commitments, deeply felt loyalties, assorted ideals and aspirations, unconscious prejudices, occasional altruism, and the usual supply of good intentions. The means by which enlightenment might be discovered through the inconsistencies and contradictions of this kind of ordinary experience are exemplified especially by what we might call the literary dimension of the Discourses—that is, the skilled and often ironic indirection through which the Buddha engages people (including the reader).

For instance, the Buddha remains always mindful that people are nurtured by the group into which they are born and to which they remain attached by deeply felt personal ties. This kind of participatory experience is humanizing and should be seen as a preparatory ground for the Buddha's higher teachings rather than an impediment to them. Not surprisingly, these higher teachings remain closely tied to the deconstructionist (or, as Thomas M. Greene says, "disjunctive") view of language that I began by noticing, aimed at freeing us from attachments and illusions. Yet, as we see, people's actual experience as participants in complex social and personal relationships needs to be addressed also by means of a more warmly engaging (let us say, again with Greene, "conjunctive")[6] and less austerely skeptical language.

And so, as historical creatures who aspire to a freedom we do not yet have and cannot adequately describe, we need to conduct our conversations vigilantly in the space between these two broad views (conjunctive and disjunctive) of how language operates. My main claim in part I is that throughout the Discourses of the Pali Canon the Buddha understands and pursues this middle way with great skill, and the dialogical example he provides in doing so remains basic to the meaning and practice of compassion, the heart of his message. In part II, I will examine how political Buddhism in Sri Lanka interprets (or fails to interpret) this aspect of the Buddha's teaching. For now, I want to turn to the main religious culture with which the Buddha engages in order to state his message, which, paradoxically, as we see, also requires a disengagement or liberation from the traditional constraints which that same culture entails. In this embeddedness of the Buddha's discourse within the Vedas, we see the dialogical process already at work and how it is inseparable from Buddhsim's self-understanding expressed either orally or in writing.

THE VEDAS:
FOUNDATIONAL TEXTS AND KEY IDEAS

There are many schools of Buddhist thought and practice, but by and large they share four basic ideas deriving from Hinduism (that is, the Vedic religious traditions from which Buddhism developed). The Sanskrit terms for these basic ideas are *anadi, karma, samsara,* and *moksa.* The first, *anadi,* means that the world has no beginning or end, but moves through cycles of creation and destruction occurring over vast stretches of time. The second, *karma,* is based on the idea that our actions are meritorious or culpable, and also that they set down memory traces predisposing us to similar kinds of behavior in the future. The third, *samsara,* is the endless round of birth, death, and rebirth in which we are caught up until we achieve the liberation indicated by the fourth term, *moksa.* In Buddhism, *moksa* is further modified by the doctrine of no-soul (*anatta*), to produce the key Buddhist concept, *nibbana.* Short of *nibbana,* people experience a wide range of attachments, desires, and responsibilities, and, within Hinduism, the doctrines of *karma* and *samsara* especially confirm the importance of our basic attachments and responsibilities to one another, and our sense of belonging in a world suffused with divine significance. The means by which ritual observance, prayer, and devout practice can assist us on our way to *moksa* are built upon the assumption, basic to Hinduism in general, that we are participants in a vast cosmic play of forces, including gods and demons, which we can to some degree influence to our advantage. Yet Buddhism would have us reject ritual and cult practice as efficacious means for adjusting the interplay between our personal *karma* (the Pali word is *kamma*) and the *samsara* we are attempting to escape. For a Buddhist, ritual in itself bears no necessary relationship to whether or not we are free from the illusions that inhibit liberation.

As we see, the Buddhist insistence on radical nonattachment pertains not only to skepticism about religious ritual, but also to skepticism about concepts and explanations. Consequently, Buddhism can make itself understood only in a provisional way, and does so especially by re-deploying the above key ideas from the Vedic tradition, its own nurturing matrix. To show what a complex negotiation this is, acknowledging a recommended (disjunctive) nonattachment on the one hand, while recognizing our many actual (conjunctive) attachments on the other, let us briefly consider some aspects of the Hindu scriptures, which themselves are complexly layered documents.

Textbook accounts of the early Vedic hymns usually connect them to an invasion of India from the north by Aryans, a people who imposed their religion, language, and culture on an already settled civilization in the Indus valley. The invasion is usually held to have occurred c. 1500 B.C.E., but whether it happened is now questioned by a broad range of scholars in various fields (philology, archaeology, history, archaeo-geography, satellite photography, among others).[7] Based on the contention that there was no invasion, a new chronology of early Indian civilization has emerged, offering drastically revised timelines—for instance, dating the *Rg Veda* at 4000 B.C.E. in contrast to the usually accepted 1400–1000 B.C.E.

Although the new theory is based on objective arguments, there are also powerful emotional and political dimensions to the repudiation of what is held to be a misguided "colonial-missionary" account that assumes that civilization must have come to India from outside—in this case, from the north and west, from where the Aryans brought their culture, language, and caste system to an indigenous population. The new theorists argue that there is no convincing evidence to support the invasion theory, and they point to changes in climate and geography to explain the major shifts in civilization for which there is good evidence.

The implications of the new theory are far-reaching, and the main points remain hotly contested, though a consensus still favors the traditional explanation. Fortunately, the controversy does not substantially affect my central concern—namely, the story of how, over time, the key insights of the early Vedic hymns developed toward a highly self-conscious, metaphysical body of writing from which, in turn, Buddhism emerged. Also, I am interested in how the path of this development is marked by a gradual relinquishment of a dominant, conjunctive view of language (and its attendant religious practices) under pressure from an analytical, disjunctive view designed to promote nonattachment. In short, participatory experience precedes critical reflection; thus, the early hymns of the *Rg Veda* express our deep interconnectedness with the universe and with one another, and remain as a prior condition for later metaphysical reflection, culminating in the *Upanishads*.

The word "Veda" (Sanskrit for "knowledge") is sometimes used in a narrow sense to describe a body of hymns and their ritual accompaniments, constituting the earliest written documents in the religious culture of ancient India.[8] But the word is also used in a broader sense to describe certain further extrapolations and reflections upon the early hymns, conducted from an increasingly philosophical point of view. As we see, *anadi* means that the world is beginningless; just so, the Vedas also are held to be without beginning or end, and are revealed in exactly the same form at each new cycle of creation. The *rsis*, or seers to whom direct vision is imparted, deploy language (*vak*) to make the eternal truth accessible in an imperfect but real way.[9] That is, words provide knowledge of the true meaning of things, and, consequently, have inherent power, leading us toward the originating mystery (*brahman*) by stages, until language itself is transcended and consumed by direct experience.

In the broad sense, the Vedas divide into four groups: *Samhita*, *Brahmana*, *Aranyaka*, and *Upanishad*. These are *sruti* ("that which has been heard"), as distinct from *smrti* ("that which has been remembered"). *Sruti* imparts revealed truth, at once primordial and eternal, whereas *smrti* depends on the status and reputation of a particular author, whose reflections upon *sruti* are judged to be cogent and illuminating.

All four collections constituting the Vedas in the broad sense are *sruti*—divine truth revealed ("heard") by the *rsis* and subsequently written down. The first collection, the *Samhita*, divides in turn into four subcollections, which constitute the Vedas in the narrow sense. These are the *Rg Veda*, *Sama Veda*, *Yajur*

Veda, and *Atharva Veda*. The *Rg Veda* is made up of hymns; the *Sama Veda* of chants or melodies; the *Yajur Veda* of ritual and sacrificial formulas; and the *Atharva Veda*, which is sometimes treated as a different kind of collection,[10] of spells and incantations. These four subcollections have in common an insistence on the foundational importance of sacrifice (*yajna*), described in the *Rg Veda* as "the world's center."[11]

The *Brahmanas* (the second division of the Vedas in the broad sense) are prose treatises describing and explaining ritual practices and their mythic antecedents and corollaries. The third collection, the *Aranyakas*, is also concerned with the sacrifice ritual, but contains further passages of philosophical and mystical reflection. The word "*Aranyakas*" means "forest books" and suggests that the compilers were exploring nontraditional teachings that might best be imparted in the safety and seclusion of a forest. If so, we have the beginnings here of an opposition between forest and village (or urban center), which will later be of considerable importance to Buddhism.

The *Upanishads* universalize the idea of liberation by thinking about it philosophically, and in so doing they challenge traditional attitudes to sacrifice. That is, by developing a set of transcendental concepts and vocabularies, the *Upanishads* call in question the efficacy of ritual for producing merit, whether to enable a propitious rebirth or to effect a final unification—as the *Upanishads* recommend—between the individual soul (*atman*) and the universal divine ground (*brahman*).

Because of the challenge they present to traditional cult practice, the *Upanishads* were at first a secret or elite teaching, and, not surprisingly, they overlap with the *Aranyakas*. Thus, the early *Brhadaranyaka Upanishad* is, as its name implies, partly an *Aranyaka*, or forest book. Yet it also retains the language of ancient sacrificial ritual, as is evident, for instance, in the remarkable opening section dealing with a horse sacrifice. In short, the philosophical self-reflexiveness of the *Upanishads* continues to evoke the language and symbolism of earlier phases of the tradition.

Although, as we see, the dates are disputed, the traditional view is that the *Rg Veda* was composed between c. 1400 and 1000 B.C.E.; the *Brahmanas* and early prose *Upanishads* (which overlap with the *Aranyakas*) between 800 and 500 B.C.E., and a later group of verse *Upanishads* between 500 and 200 B.C.E. Again, the timeline is less important for my present purposes than are developments that occur when the mythological world of the *Rg Veda* is modified and transformed by later philosophical speculation.

FROM POETRY TO PHILOSOPHY

The hymns of the *Rg Veda* emerge from a mythological background of gods, heroes, and demons not fully explained by the hymns themselves, but assumed by them. These divinities are often closely implicated, sometimes in richly inconsistent ways, with the forces of nature, and, as with the gods of ancient Greece, they pervade nature and the human observers of nature alike.

Today, educated Hindus are likely to regard the gods of the *Rg Veda* as manifestations of *brahman*, but it is difficult to ignore the polytheistic dynamism of these wonderfully various and complex divine figures, powerfully immanent in the world around us and also within ourselves. Thus, Agni, god of fire, is manifest in the natural world but is also an active principle within each human person: "Agni is head and height of heaven, the Master of earth is he," and, likewise, Agni is "shared by all men living." Similarly, Vayu is the wind but also our life-giving breath:

> Thou art our Father, Vata [Wind], yea, thou art a Brother and a
>   friend,
> So give us strength that we may live.[12]

Likewise, Indra, the main hero of the *Rg Veda*, is a divine warrior who fights with demons, chaos monsters from the deep representing both nature's destructive forces and also the archaic fears and terrors experienced at some time or other by every human person.

In short, the gods remind us that we are infused by energies that cross the boundaries between subject and object, pervading both nature and ourselves. This being the case, the sacrifice ritual is not only a means of propitiation, but also a communicative act putting us in touch with the primal energies that constitute the world and ourselves together, enabling us thereby to remake or refashion both. That is, by performing the sacrifice, we (like Indra) might be better able to ward off terror and chaos, thereby ensuring ourselves a better, longer life.

Although the word *karma* recurs some forty times in the *Rg Veda*, it is never used in connection with the idea of rebirth; rather, it indicates a sacred action or deed that may or may not be meritorious, and it is, again, connected especially to sacrifice. Basically, the Vedic sacrifice involves fire, which presumably is linked to the sun setting and rising daily from waters beneath the earth, the realm of chaos and darkness. This process of rising and setting is evident also in myriad ways throughout nature, where everything is part of an intricate web of births, deaths, and rebirths—the cosmic order (*rta*) into which the human being is woven. Indeed, everything that comes into being is, in a sense, a sacrifice because it is already given over to death—its own dissolution—as a result of which further rebirth can take place. And just as each component of nature incurs a debt by becoming individualized or separate in the first place, so this debt is paid by the eventual dissolution of every individual existence. This is as true of a raindrop as of a human being, except that the human being can grasp the process in its splendor and poignancy, and can also represent it symbolically, as in the hymns of the *Rg Veda* and the sacrificial practices informing them.

It is not difficult to see how, by further reflection, the idea of *karma* could develop in a direction emphasizing our individual human responsibility for behaving in ways that harmonize with the cosmic order, thereby reassuring us that our actions have consequences for which we are accountable and which might cause us to be reborn within the realm of *samsara*. Yet this linking of *karma* to rebirth maintains the close interweave between ourselves and the cosmos depicted already in the Vedic hymns and expressed in the prephilosophical meaning of *karma* that we find there.

Throughout the *Rg Veda*, the connection between human beings and the cosmos is further developed by a remarkable mirror imaging whereby the human not only mirrors the cosmos, but the cosmos also mirrors the human to the point, even, where the cosmos is itself depicted as a man who is sacrificed, out of whose parts the world is formed. This "primal man" (*Purusa*) is identified with the universe itself ("This Purusa is all that yet hath been and all that is to be"), and when the gods "prepared the sacrifice" they did so "with Purusa as their offering," thereby giving form to the main social strata of society:

When they divided Purusa how many portions did they make?
What do they call his mouth, his arms?
What do they call his thighs and feet?

The Brahman was his mouth, of both his arms was the Rajanya made.
His thighs became Vaisya, from his feet the Sudra was produced.

The moon was gendered from his mind, and from his eye the Sun had
    birth;
Indra and Agni from his mouth were born, and Vayu from his breath.

Forth from his navel came mid-air; they sky was fashioned from his
    head;
Earth from his feet, and from his ear the regions. Thus they formed
    the worlds.[13]

This remarkable hymn imagines the birth of the world as the sacrifice of a human being whose parts are distributed through the cosmos (moon and sun) and into human society (the four main social divisions). Later, especially in the *Brahmanas*, the primal man is identified with Prajapati, who is mentioned hardly at all in the *Rg Veda*[14] but is clearly identified in the *Brahmanas* as the primordial being. Now, however, the gods do not sacrifice Prajapati: he sacrifices himself so that the cosmos and everything in it can become manifest.[15] The sacrifice performed by humans can therefore be imagined as not only repeating the act of creation, but also as being instrumental in sustaining it.

Accounts of the sustaining aspects of sacrifice are provided especially in the *Atharva Veda* and *Brahmanas*. For instance, *Satapatha Brahmana* tells us that if the fire sacrifice is not performed properly in the morning, the sun will not rise.[16] Consequently, the fear that inspires propitiation is now accompanied by a heavy burden of responsibility: "the *agnihotra* [fire sacrifice] is unlimited and, hence, from its unlimitedness, creatures also are born unlimited."[17] In short, the sacrifice is universal, and knowing this gives us power and imposes obligations. Great prestige therefore attaches to the priestly caste, the Brahmins, whose skill and knowledge as ritual experts could shape even the "unlimited."

Not surprisingly, the idea that sacrificial ritual maintains and shapes the world developed in conjunction with the idea that the self is also shaped by the same means. That is, the correct performance of sacrifice confers merit by means of which the sacrificer attains further life, bringing to birth another body fit to dwell among the gods.[18] Thus, a person is said to be born three times: first, from parents; second, from sacrifice; third, from the funeral pyre.[19]

By suggesting in this way that we can attain to a higher life with the gods, the *Brahmanas* deemphasize the shadowy realm of the afterlife hinted at in the Vedic hymns, stressing instead an eschatological reward for well-conducted ritual observance: "so the man who performs sacrifice rids himself of his mortal body, that is to say, of sin, and by dint of verses, formulas, Vedic melodies, and offerings takes possession of the heavenly realm."[20] Yet, even those who dwell with the gods after death must eventually return to this world by rebirth,[21] and the further possibility of escaping altogether from the round of birth, death, and rebirth was not explored coherently until the topic was taken up by a group of intellectually adventurous thinkers whose conclusions are expressed in the *Upanishads*.

Again, sacrifice ritual is the key to understanding how the great metaphysical breakthrough of the *Upanishads* occurred. If, as the *Satapatha Brahmana* says, "the entire universe takes part in sacrifice,"[22] then the acquisition of knowledge is also part of the sacrificial process: "the sacrifice to Brahman" we are assured, "consists of sacred study."[23] But if sacrifice is a way of fashioning our higher selves through knowledge, then the self-sacrifice involved in gaining knowledge might turn out to be more important in the quest for liberation than the merit acquired by a ritual killing of animals. Thus, when the *Satapatha Brahmana* says that self-offerings are better than God-offerings,[24] the meaning is that sacrifices made with a view to realizing a higher self are better than material sacrifices offered to the gods. The convergence evident here between universalizing the sacrifice and interiorizing its meaning is highly significant both for the development of the *Upanishads* and for the basic ideas of Buddhism.

One way to clarify how this is so is to consider the word *brahman*. In the early Vedas it can mean a prayer or incantation with power to bring about a particular result,[25] and eventually it came also to suggest the power sustaining both the world and ourselves within it. Through proper attention to the interior sacrifice—the relinquishment, that is, of the material and egotistic self—our true, divine self, or *atman*, could realize its identity with the underlying ground, or *brahman*. The abstract formulation of this idea lies at the heart of the *Upanishads*, and is accompanied by the claim that realizing the identity of *atman* and *brahman*, with every residue of egotistic desire burnt away, frees us from *samsara*. As the *Maitri Upanishad* says, when the mind seeks after truth it comes to realize that "sense objects, / In the power of desire, are false," and "consciousness is *samsara*." Consequently:

> By the calming of consciousness
>   One kills action, both pure and impure:
> With self calmed, resting in the self
>   One wins unfailing bliss.

> If a person's consciousness
>   Were as firmly attached to *brahman*
> As it is to the sense realm,
>   Would not all be freed from bonds?[26]

The early *Brhadaranyaka* and *Chandogya Upanishads* are especially interesting in this context because their philosophical vision bears traces of earlier ideas and practices that sit uneasily with the metaphysical propositions central to the *Upanishads* as a whole. For instance, the *Brhadaranyaka Upanishad* begins with an account of the ancient Vedic horse sacrifice (I, 1), and elsewhere invokes Agni to "lead us by a good road to prosperity" (V, 15, 4). Offerings are also made for "Increasing in my own house" by way of "offspring" and "animals" (VI, 4, 24). This sounds much like the early Vedic expectation that ritual sacrifice will bring material blessings. But the *Brhadaranyaka Upanishad* also assures us that renouncers who truly know the self (*atman*) do not care for such things: "leaving behind desires for sons, for wealth, and desires for worlds, Brahmanas live in alms" (III, 5, 1); likewise, "the ancients did not desire offspring, for they thought, 'What is offspring to us, when the self (*atman*) is our world?'" (IV, 4, 22). These passages invite us to turn away from material rewards, and in so doing they focus on the self, *atman*, and its identity with *brahman*. Thus, when Yajnavalkya is asked to reveal "the *brahman* that is manifest, not hidden, that is the self within everything," he replies, "It is *your* self that is within everything" (III, 4, 2). This is the key insight, asserting a radical nondualism, explained conceptually rather than in terms of traditional ritual practices. Here is a characteristic passage:

> As a lump of rock-salt thrown into water would dissolve in the water, and there would be none, as it were, to take out again, yet wherever one took water it would be salty, so this great being, endless, boundless, consists entirely of knowledge. Having arisen from these elements, it [individuality] vanishes along with them, for after it has departed there is no consciousness. (II, 4, 12)

The main contrast in these lines is between an individual identity based on separateness ("the elements"), and the realization that our real, deepest self (*atman*) is identical with *brahman*, just as the dissolved salt becomes identical with the water. This realization comes by putting away ignorance, together with the desires, attachments, and impulses that bind us to our material existence. In turn, such a process entails a renunciation that brings us beyond duality ("the self is 'not this, not this'" [IV, 2, 4]). Here, disjunctive language ("not this, not this") helps us to understand that the path to realizing the identity of *atman* and *brahman* is based on knowledge, not ritual, and on the successful elimination of the desires and attachments that bind us to *samsara*.

The *Brhadaranyaka Upanishad* is clear about all this, insisting on the identity of *atman* and *brahman*, and also developing a new, broadly metaphysical interpretation of *karma* and rebirth. In a key passage, the Brahmin Yajnavalkya explains what happens at death, as the senses withdraw and life ebbs from the physical body. Throughout this process, the dying man "follows consciousness. His knowledge and action take hold of him, as does his former experience. As a caterpillar, reaching the end of a blade of grass and taking the next step, draws itself together, so the self, dropping the body, letting go of ignorance and taking the next step, draws itself together" (IV, 4, 2–3). The self being reborn is like a caterpillar moving from one blade of grass to another, because "as one acts, as one behaves, so does one become" (IV, 4, 5). Consequently, "When he reaches the end / Of the action he did here, / He comes back from that world / To this one, to act again" (IV, 4, 6). By contrast, "the one who does not desire, who is without desire, free from desire, whose desires are fulfilled, with the self as his desire, the breaths do not leave him. Being *brahman* he goes to *brahman*" (IV, 4, 6). To be "free from desire" requires renunciation or self-sacrifice, and by the Buddha's time, wandering ascetics were common. As we learn from the Pali Canon, they often engaged in extreme self-mortification, and Siddhatta Gotama himself became an ascetic during the early phase of his quest for enlightenment. Later, he rejected extreme self-mortification as harmful, even though he continued to advocate a moderate self-discipline in keeping with his doctrine of the middle way.

The substructure of teachings on which the Buddha drew is provided by the elements of the Vedic tradition that I have now briefly outlined, but it is worth noticing that the Buddha possibly drew also on the Samkhya[27] philosophy that developed especially under the influence of the later *Upanishads*. According to Samkhya thinking, two basic, timeless principles interpenetrate in the world of everyday experience. These are *prakrti* and *purusa*, corresponding to matter and spirit. Suffering arises from a lack of understanding that our true self is not identical with the feelings and desires associated with the ego and its bondage to the material world. As an antidote to suffering, Samkhya (the way of discrimination) calls for analysis, enabling us to become aware of the meaning of *prakrti* and its difference from *purusa*. Samkhya philosophy does not posit the existence of God, though the *Samkhyapravacana Sutra* (attributed to the founder, Kapila, who lived c. the seventh century B.C.E.) does not explicitly deny God's existence and cannot properly be called atheist.[28] As with Buddhism, "nontheist" is a more accurate description of the position espoused.

THE BUDDHA: NON-ATTACHMENT AND ENGAGEMENT

When the Buddha decided to teach others in light of his own experience of the indescribable *nibbana*, he turned to ideas, traditions, symbols, and metaphors ready at hand, adapting them to his purpose. As we see, he interprets *karma* in a highly ethical, interior way, disconnected from the ritual efficacy of sacrifice but nonetheless determining our rebirth or liberation from *samsara*. Also, he combines the ascetic ideal of renunciation (or nonattachment) with a radical internalization of the sacrifice in a manner that stresses the individual's ethical responsibility. Finally, by developing a Samkhyan type of nontheism, the Buddha takes the metaphysical vision of the *Upanishads* a step further, especially through the doctrine of *anatta*, or no-soul.

The Buddha's insistence on individual experience can return us to the general Buddhist wariness about reliance on concepts, and, in the tradition of the forest-dwelling ascetics, the Buddha teaches the relinquishment of worldly attachments. Yet, as we see, the Buddha also engages the world and would transform it in ways that mitigate suffering. As I have noticed, the Discourses of the Pali Canon are informed throughout by a carefully onsidered dialogical process involving both of these poles—the first recommending disengagement and the second requiring the opposite. Although nonattachment might well be commendable in theory, people by and large continue to be motivated by desires and feeling-structures laid down through early enculturation—mediated, in this case, through the rich, participatory sense of the world entailed by *karma*, *samsara*, and *moksa*, and their complex interconnections with the mythology, ritual, and psychology of the sacrifice. In short, the rich affective and symbolic view of the world deriving from Vedic tradition remains the soil in which the rarefied Buddhist vision is planted and is able to grow. As we see, in developing its own distinctive vision by way of an emphasis on radical nonattachment, Buddhism favors a theory of language insisting on the incommensurability of words and their referents—the disjunctive view of language I described earlier. Yet one main problem with applying such a theory in a thoroughgoing way is that it soon robs human communication of passionate life, energy, and individuality. Still, the opposite, conjunctive or participatory view of language that underpins the mythological universe of the *Rg Veda* also has drawbacks. In assuming the efficacy of language to make things happen, whether as ritual, prayer, or magic spell, this view of language soon relegates us to a world governed by priestcraft and superstition, and the breakthrough to the idea of a universal freedom that each person is responsible for seeking individually could not happen without critical detachment from conjunctive assumptions. For practical purposes, the challenge therefore lies in discovering an appropriate relationship between these two broad assessments of how language operates, neither of which alone is sufficiently sustaining.

The problem with which I am mainly concerned in the following pages arises, precisely, from a failure to discern this kind of relationship. In particular, when the aspiration to an individually realized, transcendent freedom is reinvested to promote traditional group interests and practices (as, for instance, in modern Sri Lanka), the result is a lethal contradiction through which violence is infused by a passion for the wholly unconditioned, beyond language. Tragically, such a dangerous transference can occur even despite the fact that unconditioned liberation is held to transcend group interests and practices and to entail a universal compassion. To help us to assess more clearly how this is so, I want now to turn to the Discourses of the Pali Canon, and to consider how the Buddha explores the dialogical relationship between a transcendent universalism and the cultural antecedents that, as we now see, enable its expression.

CHAPTER 2

BUDDHISM

THE ART OF THE DETACHED AGONIST

GOTAMA BUDDHA:
HISTORY AND ARCHETYPE

So far, I have proposed that Buddhism as a historical phenomenon finds expression through an extended conversation with the Vedic traditions in which it is embedded but which it also offers to transcend. As we shall see in part II, popular Buddhism in modern Sri Lanka continues to invoke a wide range of Hindu deities, and has appropriated Hindu shrines and devotional practices in order to do so. All of which can remind us that, despite the clarity of the Buddha's insistence on nonattachment, human experience by and large is a turbulent mix of desires, fears, and anxieties that need to be acknowledged and assessed.

Consequently, in engaging with modern anxieties and aspirations, the Buddha's teachings are, again, best imparted by the same kind of dialogical conversation as we find between Buddhism and the Vedas. And so it is pertinent to my main argument about modern Sri Lanka to consider how the Buddha himself deals with the complexities of ordinary human resistance to his message. But before turning to the dialogical structure of the Discourses, I want first to say a little about the life of Gotama Buddha and his central teachings.

The main events in the life of Siddhattha Gotama,[1] who became an enlightened Buddha, are generally acknowledged even across the vast range of Buddhist textual traditions, beliefs, practices, and cultures.[2] Yet the Buddha also remains elusive, not least because the individuality of the man, Gotama, is to a large extent absorbed by his archetypal identity. That is, the wise serenity and equipoise of the enlightened sage loom larger in the written texts than does the record of a human being struggling with the complexities and contradictions of history. In the

Buddha's view, historical complexities and contradictions are themselves a consequence of our habitual craving for sensory gratification; consequently, insofar as
the Pali Canon depicts the Buddha as detached, somehow above the fray, it is
telling us something about his liberated condition, unaffected by the allure of the
transient. Yet the Buddha continued to engage with his particular historical circumstances for forty-five years after Gotama's enlightenment, and during his long
preaching career, Gotama Buddha sought to tell others about the path to *nibbana*.
His engagement (or reengagement) with the world after his enlightenment en-
abled his teaching to develop as a religion (some prefer to say, a philosophy)[3]
through which, in turn, we have come to know something of the Buddha as a historical person, notwithstanding his archetypal significance.

The interplay between these two broad tendencies (the first to disengagement from history; the second to engagement with many individual people
through teaching the *Dhamma*) parallels the counterpoint I have described in the
previous chapter between disjunctive and conjunctive language, and how, despite
their opposition, each requires something of the other. Thus, the Buddha remains
disengaged from the world's turmoil because he is enlightened, and, especially in
meditation, Buddhists continue to practice this kind of detachment. Yet the Buddha also engages with the world because he has teachings to impart to the un-
awakened, who are by definition recalcitrant, wrongheaded, and confused. As I
have suggested, disjunctive language is especially effective for describing the Buddha's teachings about nonattachment; just so, his compassionate engagement
with the unenlightened requires a more familiar, conjunctive discourse. Thus, the
Buddha's assurance that each of us is an island[4] does not preclude a recognition
that we are also bound up with one another through interconnected chains of
causation—language and enculturation chief among them. Some of the Buddha's
profoundest teachings (especially in the *Suttas*, or Discourses)[5] are imparted
through a skillful management[6] of these oppositions, as, on the one hand, he
imparts something of the "prodigious heightening"[7] of his world-transforming
vision and, on the other, acknowledges common frailties and aspirations, frustra-
tions and longings, anxieties and hopes.

The Pali Canon contains no continuous narrative of the Buddha's life.
Rather, we are allowed glimpses of specific biographical events randomly distributed but not gathered into a chronological sequence. For instance, the *Mahaparinibbana Sutta* recounts the Buddha's death and final realization of *nibbana*.
Elsewhere we learn about Siddhatta's early attempts to overcome fear, and about
the ascetic phase preceding his enlightenment,[8] but there is little attempt at narrative continuity. For instance, the *Mohasaccaka Sutta* provides information about
the Buddha's early ascetic enthusiasm, and is directly preceded by the *Culasaccaka
Sutta*.[9] Yet, despite the fact that they are juxtaposed and both address Saccaka,
neither Discourse makes any reference to the other. Just so, instead of narrative

continuity, the Discourses as a whole provide us with an elaborate constellation of conversations about basic principles and insights gathered and regathered, analyzed, repeated, and expanded, without concern for systematic development. Nonetheless, a broadly familiar story about the Buddha's life has emerged from a conflation of tradition, scripture, and commentary. Thus, the enlightened Gotama is held to be one in a long line of Buddhas stretching back over aeons to his twenty-fourth predecessor, Dipankara. In turn, the Buddha of the coming age will be Maitreya, the Buddha of friendship, who will become manifest when Gotama Buddha's teaching dwindles, and when the time is right.[10]

It is uncertain when exactly the Buddha lived. In Sri Lanka and South East Asia generally, the traditional, preferred dates are 623–543 B.C.E. (thus, the 2,500th anniversary of the Buddha's final realization of *nibbana* was celebrated in 1956). Western scholars working with ancient dynastic lists and with Chinese and Tibetan translations of early (now lost) Sanskrit texts tend to prefer later dates—as late, for instance, as 480–400 B.C.E. Without entering into this debate or discussing other contending theories, we can say that the Buddha probably lived during the fifth century B.C.E., allowing for some uncertainty about the actual beginning and end of his traditionally accepted eighty-year life.[11]

At first, the Buddha's teachings were preserved orally, and were not set down in writing until the first century B.C.E., in Sri Lanka. The language used, Pali, is derived from Sanskrit and is related, though not identical with, Gotama's own language, which might have been the regional dialect of the Kingdom of Magadha.[12] The Pali Canon is the earliest surviving, complete collection from an ancient Buddhist school, and remains basic to Theravada Buddhist observance.

The Buddha himself left no written records, and his disciples committed his words to memory. Tradition has it that soon after his death, the monks held a council[13] to recite and organize what they remembered, and the first two parts of the Pali Canon (the *Vinaya Pitaka* and the *Sutta Pitaka*) were brought together and consolidated. About a century after the first council, a second council was held to resolve disputed points of doctrine and discipline. A schism occurred after the second council, dividing the conservative Sthaviravadins from more liberal Mahsanghikas. This division is usually taken as the starting point for the later development of Mahayana ("Greater Vehicle") Buddhism, as distinct from the Hinayana ("Lesser Vehicle"), sometimes identified with the Theravada ("Tradition of the Elders"). The Mahayana itself divides into various schools, and there is extensive overlap between the main Theravada and Mahayana traditions, despite their much-discussed differences. According to Theravada tradition, a third council was held during the reign of Asoka, in the third century B.C.E., to clarify authentic practice and to organize Buddhist missionary activity. At this council, a fifth book was added to a collection called the *Abhidhamma*, which was in turn incorporated into the Pali Canon.

The three main parts of the Pali Canon are known as the *Tipitaka*, or "Three Baskets," each of which contains a collection of texts. The first, the *Vinaya Pitaka*, deals with regulating the monastic life, and is about one-eighth of the collection as a whole. The second, the *Sutta Pitaka*, contains the Buddha's discourses, various popular texts, epigrams, and other miscellaneous items, and makes up roughly half of the complete collection. The third, the *Abhidhamma Pitaka*, provides an intricate philosophical and psychological analysis of the Buddha's teachings, and makes up about three-eighths of the canon. In the following pages I am concerned mainly with the *Sutta Pitaka* (the Discourses) because these show clearly the complexity and dialogical subtlety of the Buddha's teaching practice. But let us now return briefly to the Buddha's biography.

Siddhatta Gotama was born into the Sakya clan, just north of the Indian border in modern Nepal. His father was Suddhodana, a ruler of Kapilavatthu, which was governed along republican lines rather than as a monarchy, such as the states to the south that would later offer patronage to the Buddha. Gotama's mother, Maya, died one week after giving birth, and Gotama was raised by his mother's sister, Prajapati, who became his father's second wife. At age sixteen, he married Yasodhara, with whom he had a son, Rahula.

From childhood, Gotama led a protected life because his father did not want him to see how much suffering there was in the world. But despite his father's well-intentioned vigilance, the young Gotama happened upon a lame old man, a leper ravaged by disease, and a funeral procession. From these experiences he learned that old age, disease, and death are the human lot, and in light of his new knowledge he examined his own privileged life, which he decided to renounce. And so he secretly left his sleeping wife and child and became a wandering ascetic, embracing homelessness in his search for release from *samsara*, to which, he now realized, humans are condemned unless they find a way to liberate themselves.

Gotama was instructed by two teachers, Alara Kalama and Uddaka Ramaputta, who taught him meditation techniques (probably based on yoga) that have remained a staple of Buddhist practice. It seems that Alara Kalama also taught a form of Samkhya philosophy that, as we have seen, developed from the *Upanishads* and was nontheist. That is, it did not posit a creator God or require the existence of God for salvation. Rather, it called for discrimination as a means of understanding how material nature (*prakrti*) everywhere contains and conceals the spirit (*purusa*). Suffering occurs when discrimination fails, and we find ourselves trapped by materiality instead of liberated through the spirit.

Although Gotama retained some elements of what he had learned from his teachers, he struck out on his own and became an ascetic for a period of six years, hoping that extreme austerity would enable him to discover the enlightenment he sought. Eventually, he concluded that asceticism was not the answer, and he began to eat properly and to tend to his physical well-being.

A group of five ascetics with whom he had been acquainted were offended by Gotama's behavior, and turned away from him. But Gotama had realized that neither the luxury of his early upbringing nor the intense self-denial of his ascetic years was the answer. Rather, he should pursue a middle way between these extremes.

Proceeding alone, Gotama spread grass under a tree (later known as the Bodhi tree) and promised that he would meditate until he found enlightenment. Despite temptations by Mara (the lord of this world, and also a representation of everything in one's own nature resistant to enlightenment), Gotama attained *nibbana*.

Now a Buddha or "awakened one," Gotama at first did not think to teach others, but was persuaded to do so by the god Brahma.[14] The Buddha then sought out the five former companions who had rejected him, and who were now instantly won over by his implicit authority. In his first sermon, delivered at Benares and later known as the Sermon in the Deer Park, the Buddha taught the Four Noble Truths, and thereby set the wheel of the *Dhamma* in motion.

As his followers multiplied, so also the Buddha's instructions developed in complexity as he gathered together the *Sangha*—that is, the community of monks, *bhikkhus*, and eventually nuns, *bhikkhunis*. For the next forty-five years, he continued to travel and to teach, especially in the monarchies of Magadha and Kosala, where King Bimbisara and King Pasenadi offered him protection and patronage.

The Buddha's death occurred in the company of Ananda, at the small town of Kusinara. The Buddha had fought off an illness, but soon afterward he was poisoned by food received from an almsgiver (Cunda, the smith). As he died, realizing *nibbana* (the "*nibbana* without remainder" because he would not return to a human body), the earth shook: "Terrible was the quaking, men's hair stood on end / When the all-accomplished Buddha passed away."

As with the Sermon in the Deer Park at Benares with which the Buddha's preaching career began, the Discourse describing his death was preserved orally and underwent the same process of modification as did the Buddha's teachings as a whole, in response to the need for clarity and pedagogical effectiveness. Evidence of a long period of oral transmission is immediately obvious even to a casual reader of the Pali Canon, in which formulaic set pieces and lists are repeated frequently. One result of these carefully elaborated repetitions is a sense of stability that offsets and contains the variety of arguments that the Buddha's challengers, as well as his misunderstanding followers, bring against him. Despite the fact that each individual person must find liberation alone (as did Gotama), clear instructions and frequently repeated guidelines provide a map to guide us along the way. In the Pali Canon, the basic coordinates of this map are frequently set out, and constitute the main tenets of what Buddhism is taken to be.

THE MAIN TEACHINGS: NEGOTIATING
NON-ATTACHMENT AND ENGAGEMENT

Standard accounts of what the Buddha taught usually begin with the Four Noble Truths. These are: (1) The Noble Truth of Suffering; (2) The Origin of Suffering; (3) The Ending of Suffering; (4) The Path Leading to the Ending of Suffering (that is, the Noble Eightfold Path).[15] The word for "suffering" here is *dukkha*, which carries the further connotations of "emptiness," "impermanence," "dissatisfaction," and even of a wheel out of kilter (that is, there is something basically awry that upsets the smooth running of things).[16] The source of *dukkha*, to which the second Noble Truth directs us, is craving (*tanha*), which has the connotation of "thirst," "desire," "greed." Craving describes not only our impulses toward sensual gratification, but also our attachment to ideas, concepts, and beliefs—including even the idea of liberation. The third Noble Truth offers assurance that *dukkha* can cease, as it does when *tanha* is extinguished. When this occurs, "It is liberated," and in this context the word "*nibbana*" points to the ultimate value about which nothing substantial can be said. Although *nibbana* is sometimes compared to the idea of extinguishing or "blowing out" (as of a candle), and also of cooling (as with the abating of a fever), it is not caused by anything and one does not enter into it as a state or condition, because all conditioned things pass away. Consequently, *nibbana* is not described adequately as a fever cooled or a flame gone out: these metaphors might indirectly describe some consequences of leaving behind all clinging, craving, and attachments, but we are repeatedly made aware in such discussions that language is used disjunctively, pointing to something that exceeds its grasp. Moreover, because *nibbana* is entirely unconditioned, no description of it can fail to be misleading. As the *Asankhatasamyutta* says: "Thus, bhikkhus, I have taught you the unconditioned and the path leading to the unconditioned. . . . This is our instruction to you."[17] But the Buddha says very little about this "unconditioned," partly because it is the cessation of suffering, and we need to attend first to the practical tasks of extinguishing the craving at the root of suffering everywhere around us.

The Buddha's famous Fire Sermon directs us to this practical task by singling out greed, hatred, and delusion as the three "fires" that are the chief manifestations of craving (*tanha*). The Fire Sermon, which stands deliberately in contrast to the Brahmin fire-sacrifice, presents the Buddha as a physician who cures his disciples of the pains of "birth, aging, and death" as he brings them to realize, "It's liberated."[18] In short, the aim is practical, and speculation about what it means to be liberated is less important than curing the disease. Thus, in a favorite parable, the Buddha asks if a man struck by a poisoned arrow will be concerned with who shot it, what kind of bow was used, how the bow was strung, and so on.[19] No: the main thing is to remove the arrow and to heal the wound. So it is with *tanha*, the craving that poisons us; its extinction is *nibbana*, which is realized when we are cured. Meanwhile, the means by which the cure is effected are stated in the fourth Noble Truth, which directs us to the Noble Eightfold Path.

The Noble Eightfold Path[20] is a set of guidelines comprising: (1) right view; (2) right intention; (3) right speech; (4) right action; (5) right livelihood; (6) right effort; (7) right mindfulness; (8) right concentration. The implications of these eight directives are analyzed in detail at various points in the Pali Canon, opening up in turn upon a further range of subdivisions. Among these subdivisions is a recurrent and important description of four stages by which we might arrive at a final liberation from *samsara*.[21] The first, "stream-enterer," occurs at the crucial moment when we awaken to the *Dhamma*, as a result of which we discard doubts, attachment to rituals and to the idea of personality (that is, the idea of an independent, substantial self). A stream-enterer is subject to further rebirths, but will attain *nibbana* after no more than seven of these. At the second stage we find the "once-returner," who will attain *nibbana* after one rebirth. Third is the "nonreturner," who will not be reborn in this world after death, but will attain *nibbana* in one of the higher realms. At the fourth stage is the *arahant*, who has destroyed all cravings and will attain final *nibbana* "without remainder" at death.

As these divisions suggest, the way to liberation can span many lifetimes. It is a process in which we are complexly involved through our *kammic* history— the dance of illusion and desire extending across the vast stretches of time in which *samsara* involves us. It follows that when an *arahant* attains *nibbana*, a series of rebirths stretching back beyond our capacity to imagine, is discontinued. This sense of a deep interinvolvement—"interbeing," as Thich Nhat Hanh[22] calls it—is of great significance to Buddhism and to the compassion it enjoins, and it is closely connected to the further key Buddhist doctrine of Dependent Origination.

The Chain of Dependent Origination (*Paticca-samuppada*) describes how we are bound into suffering because of our ignorance of the Four Noble Truths and how, consequently, we are unable to break the chain of cause and effect that condemns us to rebirth. The main links in this chain are usually classified as a sequence of twelve, as in the following passage:

> So, bhikkhus, with ignorance as condition, formations [come to be]; with formations as condition, consciousness; with consciousness as condition, mentality-materiality; with mentality-materiality as condition, the sixfold base; with the sixfold base as condition, contact; with contact as condition, feeling; with feeling as condition, craving; with craving as condition, clinging; with clinging as condition, being; with being as condition, birth; with birth as condition, ageing and death, sorrow, lamentation, pain, grief, and despair come to be. Such is the origin of this whole mass of suffering.[23]

The "whole mass of suffering" with which this passage ends is the empirical reality of our day-to-day world, and by working back up the chain, we can understand how this state of affairs has come to be. Thus, our immediate grief and suffering are caused by the fact that we age and die as a consequence of having been born. In turn, birth is conditioned by desires to which we cling because of the *kammic* burden of our past actions. That to which we cling is then reborn, and shapes the new consciousness arising in the womb. This consciousness in turn takes on a physical form, the *nama-rupa* ("name-and-form"), the basic psychophysical entity that engages the world through our six senses (sight, hearing, smell, taste, touch, and mind). When the senses have contact with their appropriate object, feeling arises and becomes the source of the craving that enthralls us as we reenter *samsara*.

The Chain of Dependent Origination is entailed by the Four Noble Truths and helps to conceptualize the process by which we are reborn into the illusion and suffering that constitute our historical reality. But what is reborn is not a substantive self; rather, the cluster of habits and desires that must continue on the carousel of *samsara* until they are extinguished. However, if there is no substantial self—no *atman*—then what does it mean, for instance, to say that the Buddha remembers his past lives (as he claims to do)?[24]

This is not an easy question to answer, and the Pali Canon is, to say the least, uncomfortable about it. As we have seen, even the stream-enterer must lay aside "personality belief," the notion of a substantive self. Yet this does not mean that there are no persons or no selves; the conventional terms we use from day to day to describe one another remain useful for practical purposes. Buddhism frequently draws a distinction between conventional and ultimate truth, and although it is often convenient to refer to a certain "person" or to use the word "self," if we examine the content of "person" and "self" analytically, we will not find any entity corresponding to the conventional term. As Nagasena says, when a chariot is broken down into its component parts, the chariot ceases to exist. So it is with the self. It is an aggregate, merely, of the bits and pieces that make it up. Like the chariot, the self is no more than an assemblage of parts and does not have an existence separate from them. The name for these component parts is *khandhas*, and there are five of them:[25] material form, feeling, perception, mental formations, and consciousness. They overlap with the categories described in the Chain of Dependent Origination and they are conditions that we experience in our repeated rebirth and suffering.

Still, the question presses:[26] Who or what is reborn? As we see, the answer cannot be that a substantive self survives, though in popular Buddhism the doctrine of rebirth is often imagined in this way. Such a thing cannot happen because the aggregates (like the parts of the chariot) fall apart and disperse at death. Yet *kammic* patterns endure in the form of the habits that have shaped consciousness, and in the desires and clinging that make consciousness an impediment to *nibbana*. These *kammic* patterns reenter the cycle, rather as a wave reenters the ocean and is remanifested as another wave, neither identical to nor different from its predecessors. If a candle is used to light another candle, the new flame is not the same, nor is it entirely different from the old. Similes such as these are often used to help us to imagine a middle way between annihilation and enduring identity, but, as ever, the Buddha is careful to guard against the imprecision of language, and he refuses to answer when he is asked whether or not there is a self. The Buddha explains to Ananda that if he had said "There is a self," then "that would have been siding with those ascetics and Brahmins who are eternalists." But if he had said, "There is no self," then "this would be siding with those ascetics and Brahmins who are annihilationists."[27] So the Buddha remains silent as the best means, in the circumstances, of having his interlocutor understand that some questions cannot be answered clearly. In a further dialogue, the Buddha refuses to answer a set of closely allied questions of a similarly speculative kind, having to do with such issues as the eternity of the world and what happens to the Tathagata (a title for the Enlightened One, meaning "Gone There") after death. These questions are the *avyakatani* or indeterminates, the "undecided points," so called because the Buddha consistently refuses to address them directly. They are: Is the world eternal or not? Is the world infinite or not? Is the soul the same as the body or not? Does the Tathagata exist, not exist, both exist and not exist, neither exist nor not exist after death? The Buddha tells his interlocutor, Vacchagotta, that such questions are "speculative," and "something the Tathagata has put away." When Vacchagotta then declares himself bewildered, the Buddha offers him little respite: "It is enough to cause you bewilderment, Vaccha, enough to cause you confusion. For this Dhamma, Vaccha, is profound, hard to see and hard to understand, peaceful and sublime, unattainable by mere reasoning, subtle, to be experienced by the wise."[28] By implication, if Vaccha were wiser, more subtle, peaceful, and sublime, he wouldn't ask in the first place. And so we return to the idea implicit in the metaphor of the man wounded by a poisoned arrow. The task at hand is to attend to the wound, rather than ask idle questions about the archer.

The Buddha's reticence on the undeclared points is offset by the explicitness and insistence with which the Chain of Dependent Origination is declared throughout the canon, promoting, as it does, the idea that *kammic* formations shape the consciousness that endures rebirth (or remanifestation). That is, we are responsible moral agents, and the moral vision of Buddhism extends to and entails the liberation of all suffering creatures with whose state and condition each of us is bound up. If we are responsible for the *kamma* we accumulate during our earthly lifetimes, then some degree of continuity is necessary to explain the moral dimension of rebirth. If there is no soul, it becomes difficult to explain this continuity, and this is a difficulty that cannot just be dismissed as idle speculation.

Understandably, popular Buddhism has gone on imagining rebirth as individual survival, more or less ignoring the intellectual subtleties and austere disjunctive language of the learned expositors of *anatta*.[29] Perhaps our deep desire to propagate ourselves genetically is mirrored in our persistent beliefs about personal survival after death. Certainly, at the popular level, many Buddhists find that a thoroughgoing disjunctive approach to such matters is somehow counterintuitive, and they seek instead for more reassuring, positive ways of imagining. One such way is supplied by a common-stock idea widely disseminated in Hindu culture, maintaining that a dying person's last thought is the first connecting link to rebirth. The modern Sri Lankan Buddhist, Walpola Rahula, explains: "the last thought-moment in this life conditions the first thought-moment in the so-called next life, which, in fact, is the continuity of the same series. During this life itself, too, one thought-moment conditions the next thought-moment. So from the Buddhist point of view, the question of life after death is not a great mystery, and a Buddhist is never worried about this problem." Rahula also assures us that the person dies and is reborn "is neither the same person, nor another,"[30] thus preserving the paradoxical denial of both continuity and discontinuity that led the Buddha to maintain a tactful silence on the topic.

The moment of connection between death and rebirth is often further imagined by way of a slightly unnerving combination of literalism and fantasy. For the connecting link to occur, the *kamma*-laden consciousness of the dead person, hungry for rebirth, is imagined as seeking for an appropriate copulating couple. The woman must be at a fertile time, the sex act must take place, and the linking-consciousness must be ready to intervene. Only then can conception occur. A mythological figure called the *gandhabba* is adapted to explain the process. The *gandhabba* was originally a celestial spirit associated with the primal waters that preexisted the creation, and also with birth from the womb. Subsequently, as Collins explains, the *gandhabba* was identified with the "being seeking rebirth," or "the being about to enter the womb."[31] The process is described in the *Mahatanhasankhya Sutta*,[32] which begins with Sati, son of a fisherman, proclaiming that "it is this same consciousness that runs and wanders through the round of rebirths" (349). The Buddha is rather sharp with Sati, reminding him that consciousness is "dependently arisen," as the Buddha has pointed out in "many discourses." By misunderstanding this, "you, misguided man, have misrepresented us by your wrong grasp and injured yourself and stored up much demerit; for this will lead to your harm and suffering for a long time" (350). The Buddha goes on to explain the Chain of Dependent Origination, and includes an account of rebirth:

> Bhikkhus, the conception of an embryo in a womb takes place through the union of three things. Here, there is the union of the mother and father, but it is not the mother's season, and the being to be reborn [the

gandhabba] is not present—in this case there is no conception of an embryo in a womb. Here, there is the union of the mother and father, and it is the mother's season, but the being to be reborn is not present— in this case too there is no conception of an embryo in a womb. But when there is the union of the mother and father, and it is the mother's season, and the being to be reborn is present, through the union of these three things the conception of an embryo in a womb takes place. (358)[33]

As we see, the Discourse opens with the Buddha's impatience with the for-lorn Sati who, we are told, "sat silent, dismayed, with shoulders drooping and head down, glum, and without response" (350). We might detect here some suggestion that Sati's question was common, and even though the Buddha ad-dressed it in "many discourses," people keep bringing it up. Sati is rebuked, even threatened (his mistake will cause him to suffer for "a long time") and he is so crestfallen that readers (or listeners) are less likely to repeat his mistake. All of which might suggest that there is, indeed, a certain uncomfortable self-consciousness here about the difficulty of the point to be made. As we see, the doctrine of *anatta* calls upon a strongly disjunctive use of language; yet we need also to know how personal responsibility is carried across numerous rebirths, and some kind of conjunctive account is helpful for describing how this occurs. The imagined, voyeuristic *gandhabba* looking for a likely copulating couple pro-vides such an account, its strange materiality offsetting the conceptual difficulty of explaining that although there is no soul, something nonetheless is remani-fested if we die without having realized *nibbana*. Our habitual cravings, our *kammically* conditioned desires are reassembled within the *samsaric* routine, but the ego or self of the person who has died does not survive, somehow intact. When an *arahant* realizes *nibbana*, so too a whole history of preceding rebirths comes to an end. It follows that we do not save ourselves alone (not least be-cause there are no alone selves to save), and if I remember a former life, it is more like remembering another person than of somehow recognizing myself (my present "name-and-form") displaced, say, into another era.

I have concentrated on the difficult question of *anatta* in connection to the idea of rebirth because certain core values of Buddhism, as with any other sys-tem of belief, are declared especially clearly through the main contradictions and conceptual difficulties that such systems encounter. It is as if the will to be-lieve becomes clearest when the reasons to believe are most obscure. As we see, the Buddha's revolutionary development of the *Upanishads* in the direction of an irreducible human self-determination sits uneasily with traditional concepts such as *atman*, *karma*, and *samsara*, on which the Buddha nonetheless draws to make himself understood, and also to enable him to express the idea that we are bound up with one another in unimaginably far-reaching ways. Everywhere, the Discourses draw attention to the Buddha's dependence on traditions that he also offers to transcend, and we are asked to respond discerningly to a sustained interplay between extraordinary nonattachment and ordinary engagement. The degree to which the Discourses draw attention to their own language as a means of exemplifying and promoting such discernment is remarkable but also insufficiently observed, which is why I now want to say a little more about it.

THE DISCOURSES:
USE AND ABUSE OF LANGUAGE

In the *Kandaraka Sutta*,[34] the Buddha offers instruction to a wandering ascetic, Kandaraka. In the course of the dialogue, the Buddha also criticizes the Brahmin sacrifice ritual for imposing unnecessary suffering on the sacrificial animals and on their suppliers. Toward the end of the Discourse, the Buddha praises people who refrain from inflicting torment on themselves or others, and he explains how the good behavior of such people is mirrored in their speech. Thus, a *bhikkhu* who is on the right path eschews "false speech," "malicious speech," and "harsh speech" (449). Also, "he does not repeat elsewhere what he has heard in order to divide [those people] from these," and he is "a speaker of words that promote concord"; that is, he "speaks such words as are gentle, pleasing to the ear, and loveable, as go to the heart, are courteous, desired by many and agreeable to many" (449). In short, false, malicious, and harsh speech adds to suffering in much the same way as do violent sacrificial practices, extreme asceticism, and the exploitation of workers. By contrast, the promotion of "concord" by means of "courteous" language is the way of a *bhikkhu* who lives in the spirit of the *Dhamma*, and who "speaks at the right time, speaks what is fact, speaks on what is good" (449).

This emphasis on speaking "at the right time" recurs frequently in the Discourses and draws attention to the importance of gauging correctly what kind of speech will best promote harmony. Good timing and the ability to choose words that will "go to the heart" are not specifiable by rule, but are exemplified by the art of the Buddha's own conduct and language. Clearly stated doctrines indeed remain important, but they do not sufficiently engage the feelings and prejudices that are the source of people's misunderstanding and ignorance. This insufficiency is partly supplied by the personal example of those living in the spirit of the *Dhamma*, and the *Kandaraka Sutta* calls attention specifically to the importance of courteous language as a means of promoting the quest for liberation in a complex and difficult world.

Advice about the proper use of language is offered also in the *Cula-hatthipadopama Sutta*,[35] in which the Buddha describes spiritual progress by comparing a disciple to a woodsman tracking an elephant. At one point, the

Buddha considers the difference between proper and improper speech, and uses exactly the same passage about courteous language as in the *Kandaraka Sutta*. Clearly, this is a set piece, repeated because of its usefulness in addressing a perennially important issue.

Again, in the *Bahuvendaniya Sutta*,[36] the Buddha discusses different types of feeling, and notices that although he has set out the *Dhamma* clearly, "it may be expected that those who will not concede, allow, and accept what is well stated and well spoken" will fall into quarrels and disputes, "stabbing each other with verbal daggers" (503). By contrast, those who do accept what is well spoken will live in concord and view one another "with kindly eyes" (503). Here, a failure to understand and accept the *Dhamma* merely perpetuates violence and suffering ("quarrels and disputes"), including, not least, violent and abusive language, the opposite of the courteous discourse that promotes harmony.

The topic of verbal dispute or "wordy warfare"[37] is taken up again in the *Pasadika Sutta*, which deals with differences between good and bad teachers. The Discourse begins by drawing attention to an argument following the death of Nigantha Nataputta, the Jain leader. The unedifying behavior of Nataputta's followers leads to a further discussion in which the Buddha intervenes. First, he says, the Jain leader was not fully enlightened, and that is the root of the problem because an enlightened teacher imparts a doctrine that is "well-proclaimed" and "edifyingly displayed" (428). The Buddha then announces the preeminence of his own teaching, and gives advice about how to deal properly with disputes. He says that people should not reject or disparage, but explain "the correct meaning and expression" (432). Later, he says that the Tathagata especially "knows the right time to reply" (436), and certain questions should not be raised because they are "not conducive to welfare or to the Dhamma" (437).

The polemical aspect of this Discourse is obvious from the opening paragraphs describing internecine quarrels among the Jains, and from the Buddha's confidence in his own teaching. But attention focuses also on the harmony of "meaning and expression," and on the choice to intervene or to keep silent. Here, again, the Discourse calls attention to how the deployment of complex language represents and embodies a spirit of understanding that remains central to the effective promulgation of the *Dhamma* itself.

As we see from these examples, it is important to choose the right moment to intervene because people are not in all circumstances equally open to receiving the information they need, or to hearing it in a way that will bear fruit. Consequently, throughout the Discourses, the Buddha deploys a variety of linguistic strategies for dealing with a wide range of interlocutors.

For instance, although the Buddha "speaks at the right time what is correct and to the point,"[38] on certain occasions he can speak harshly. Sometimes, "overt sharp speech" might be appropriate, and "one may utter it, knowing the time to do so." At one point, the Buddha describes himself as conducting conversations as if he were a charioteer who knows the parts of the chariot and can answer questions about them without hesitation, "on the spot."[39] That is, rather than withdraw from a contingent world of false appearances and impermanence, he engages such a world more effectively than other people by being sensitive to its changeability, its moments of opportunity, and the many ways in which people dwell within it. Such skill and discernment are exemplified by the rhetorical diversity of the Discourses themselves, as the Buddha not only imparts clear instructions about the ordering of the good life, but also offers examples to show how these instructions might actually engage with the greed, hatred, and delusions of a *kamma*-laden world inhabited by a menagerie of human types for whom clearly imparted doctrine will have insufficient appeal.

As we have seen, by insistently individualizing the moral life, the Buddha enjoins people to strive for truth by their own lights, working toward it by way of experience and intelligent inquiry, rather than by conformity to group practice, religious or otherwise. Thus, in a much-quoted passage, the Buddha advises his disciples that each is an island, which is to say, self-reliant in the quest for truth:

> Therefore, Ananda, you should live as islands unto yourselves, being your own refuge, with no one else as your refuge. . . . And how does a monk live as an island unto himself . . . with no other refuge? Here, Ananda, a monk abides contemplating the body as body, earnestly, clearly aware, mindful and having put away all hankering and fretting for the world.[40]

The dialogical form of the Discourses as a whole is especially useful for conveying how truth is, as this passage would have us understand, a process of discovery by a self-sufficient, responsible human agent "with no other refuge," rather than a consequence of belief in received practices, priestly mediation, or ritual observance. Consequently, dialogue remains at the core of the Buddha's teaching insofar as it enables a compassionate understanding of how individual people struggle with their own *kamma*, prejudices, and habits of thought as they attempt to grapple with the *Dhamma* and its implications.

Still, clearly stated doctrine is also important. As we have seen, the Buddha is supremely confident about his authority and does not hesitate to affirm that "whatever he proclaims, says or explains is so and not otherwise."[41] The pounding repetitiveness of key ideas, the insistent classifications and systematizing of doctrinal points remain front and center, reminding us of the Buddha's radical ethicizing of the moral life, the radical insubstantiality of the self, and the importance of nonattachment. These teachings are austere, demanding, and imperative, and they remain the conceptual core of Buddhism, stressing the singular interiority of experience beyond allegiance to kin-group, caste, nation, religious cult, or, indeed, any attachment whatsoever. As we see, in imparting such teachings, the Buddha is neither withdrawn from the world with which he has chosen to engage, nor is he caught up in the world's *samsaric* illusion. Rather, he releases into the world a transformative energy, and the Discourses especially dramatize the interplay between precept and practice through which the power of a living *Dhamma* is best expressed. The treatment of Ananda (the Buddha's cousin and personal attendant) in the *Mahaparinibbana Sutta*[42] provides a good example of this dialogical interplay at work.

As the Buddha nears death, he offers a summary of his key teachings, including a "comprehensive discourse" (235) on morality in which he sets out the Four Noble Truths, the Noble Eightfold Path, and the Four Stages of Liberation, before going on to describe various perils typically encountered along the way. He also provides instructions for the *Sangha* after he is gone, and makes his funeral arrangements. In the course of all this he repeats the familiar metaphors comparing each of us to an island (we must strive alone) (245), and comparing his teaching to a raft (it can be discarded when it gets us to shore) (239). Throughout, he remains unperturbed about his impending death, and even chooses (against the blandishments of Mara) the moment at which he will renounce the life principle and realize final *nibbana*.

This mixture of elements is in itself unexceptional, and yet the *Mahaparinibbana Sutta* is a strangely moving document, not least because the Buddha chose to spend his final days in the small, out-of-the-way town of Kusinara, attended at last only by the faithful Ananda. The indignity of his being poisoned by bad food (the cause of his death) is offset by the dignity with which he endures his ordeal and by his consideration for the hapless smith, Cunda, who fed him. The Buddha assures Ananda that Cunda should not be remorseful because the most meritorious almsgivings are those directly preceding the Tathagata's enlightenment and his final passing (261). There is some rueful compassion in Cunda thus being made to feel especially meritorious for having killed the Buddha, but the fullest complexity of the Discourse becomes evident in the characterization of Ananda.

As we see, Ananda has to have explained to him that Cunda is not to blame. For the Buddha, intention alone is morally significant, and Ananda needs to be reminded of this. Here we should recall that although Ananda was the Buddha's personal attendant, he did not attain enlightenment before the Buddha died, though he did before his own death. Consequently, Ananda is still in the process of finding his way, and is likely to misunderstand and to maintain attachments that would be impossible for an *arahant*. Thus, he is kindly, attentive, and intelligent, but frequently he misses the point, and he is not quite in control of his emotions.

From the start, Ananda has a way of getting things wrong, as, for instance, when he asks the Buddha about the rebirths of particular individuals. The Buddha replies by setting out the four levels of liberation (stream-enterer, once-returner, no-returner, *nibbana* directly attained), and then reproves Ananda for asking the wrong question: "Ananda, it is not remarkable that that which has come to be as a man should die. But that you should come to the Tathagata to ask the fate of each of those who have died, that is a weariness to him" (241). There is some exasperation in this response, though the Buddha does not specify the flaw in Ananda's thinking (that he holds to a view of continued personal identity without considering *anatta*). Rather, Ananda's question enables the Buddha to set out the fourfold scheme for our, and Ananda's, edification, while reminding us that knowing the doctrine does not mean that we see its implications fully, as we, like Ananda, stumble along our own uncertain path.

Later in the Discourse, the Buddha explains that he could easily "live for a century, or the remainder of one" (246). Here we are to recall that the Buddha is eighty years old (245), and that a full lifespan was held to be one hundred years. The implication is that Ananda only has to ask and the Buddha will agree to live for the full span, but the unfortunate Ananda misses the point:

> the venerable Ananda, failing to grasp this broad hint, this clear sign, did not beg the Lord: "Lord, may the Blessed Lord stay for a century, may the Well-Farer stay for a century for the benefit and happiness of the multitude, out of compassion for the world, for the benefit and happiness of devas and humans," so much was his mind possessed by Mara. (246)

Ananda fails to see his opportunity; he does not take the hint, and the result is that the Buddha renounces the life-principle and commits himself to die in three months. Later, Ananda does ask the Buddha to remain, but the request is met with some impatience: "Enough, Ananda! Do not beg the Tathagata, it is not the right time for that!" The Buddha then makes himself painfully explicit:

> Then, Ananda, yours is the fault, yours is the failure that, having been given such a broad hint, such a clear sign by the Tathagata, you did not understand and did not beg the Tathagata to stay for a century.... If, Ananda, you had begged him, the Tathagata would twice have refused you, but the third time he would have consented. Therefore, Ananda, yours is the fault, yours is the failure. (251–52)

The Buddha repeats the point, rubbing it in, and ends by saying that now it "is not possible" (253) for him to change his mind and live longer.

We are not told what the wretched Ananda thought about being accused of such a momentous "fault" and "failure." We are told that "his mind" was "possessed by Mara," and we might recall how, at Gotama's enlightenment, Mara also intervened and was dispelled by the Buddha, who was then persuaded by Brahma to bring his teaching to the world. This key event in the Buddha's life is echoed here in reverse, which helps to explain why the account is so protracted, and how strangely it reads. Mara has blunted Ananda's discernment, and Ananda fails to make an equivalent request to Brahma's. The result is that as the Buddha departs from the world, his final *nibbana* counterpoints his entry into *nibbana* at the moment of Gotama's enlightenment. The story is poignant in reminding us that the Buddha's lifespan is limited, but also that the Buddha's engagement with the world depends on his own discernment of the need and opportunity at hand. By contrast, Ananda's lapse in discernment is (as we are told) a failure of timing, of being unable to read the moment's opportunity. Recognizing the *Buddha-Dhamma* amid the complexities of daily life remains a challenge for us as much as for Ananda, and if Mara addles our brains, binding us in the nets of attachment and desire, we too will go on missing the opportunity, in a way that the Buddha did not.

The dialogue with Ananda takes yet a further turn as the Buddha encourages him to "make the effort" (265) because he has already stored much merit, and in a short time will attain liberation. The Buddha then praises Ananda for (of all things) a good sense of timing: "He knows when it is the right time for monks to come to see the Tathagata, when it is the right time for nuns, for male lay-followers" (265). Yet, directly after receiving this praise and encouragement, Ananda puts his foot in it again, by questioning the Buddha's choice to retire to Kusinara, a "miserable little town of wattle-and-daub, right in the jungle in the back of beyond" (266). Once more, the Buddha has to set Ananda right, informing him that Kusinara was formerly an important capital city and in its present condition is an appropriate place for the Buddha to take his departure. The Buddha's main point is that worldly kingdoms are impermanent, but there is some poignancy in his decision to stay alone, except for Ananda, in this out-of-the-way location, his dying all but unnoticed.

The Buddha's praise of Ananda for effectively organizing the monks, nuns, and lay followers reminds us that Ananda is ready to assume an important role in the *Sangha* once the Buddha departs. But no sooner has the Buddha corrected him on the significance of Kusinara than the hapless Ananda commits yet another error of judgment by refusing to admit the wandering ascetic, Subhadda, into the Buddha's presence. Understandably, Ananda wants to protect the ailing Buddha, who finds it necessary to overrule his zealous disciple and to allow Subhadda an interview. It seems that Ananda's organizational skills and ability to judge "the right time" are not flawless. He may do better than most, but he won't get things quite right, and we ought not to expect perfection even from the best-intentioned and talented of administrators. This is a lesson not just for Ananda, but for the *Sangha* as a whole.

When the Buddha dies, we are told that some *bhikkhus* "who had not yet overcome their passions" tore their hair and threw themselves down in grief. By contrast, "those monks who were free from craving endured mindfully" (272), making dispassionate observations on the impermanence of things. This second group is detached and remains calm, yet the overtly grieving *bhikkhus* are somehow more humanly agreeable than their chilly brethren whose lack of emotion is unsettling. The fact that we think this might merely indicate that we, too, are overburdened by attachments, and if we were further along the road to enlightenment we might admire the dispassionate *bhikkhus* as the truly wise ones. Perhaps, but that is something we would have to take on faith because most of us, meanwhile, might prefer the company of the grieving ones, and of the imperfect Ananda.

Throughout this interesting Discourse, we are reminded that vigilance, timing, and attentive engagement are basic to the *Dhamma*, even though these qualities cannot be described or schematized like the Four Noble Truths and the Noble Eightfold Path. As we see, the Discourse comes especially alive through the characterization of Ananda, and in the interplay between our unproblematic understanding of the Buddha's teachings stated in propositional form, and our more ambivalent sympathy for his unenlightened disciple, finding his way with difficulty. As we see, the friendly, capable, and solicitous Ananda keeps missing the point and is reproved for his failures, even as his talents are acknowledged and praised. Our response to Ananda forces us then to make complex judgments. Should he not have known better than to ask about the rebirths of individuals? Should he be blamed for not having persisted in asking the Buddha three times to live for another twenty years? Should he not have seen the significance of the Buddha's choice of Kusinara? Was he wrong to protect the ailing Buddha from the importunate Subhadda? Although the Buddha provides directives on how to think about such questions, we, like Ananda, might find ourselves struggling for clarity in response to them. Our ambivalence is then deepened by the episode of Cunda the smith, who is praised despite the fact that he kills the Buddha, and also in the concluding section on the grieving monks and their chilly brethren. Throughout, we are aware of contrary impulses at work shaping our judgment, and the self-conscious arrangement of these episodes indicates how the Discourse is designed to have us experience something of the asymmetrical relationship between precept and practice. Although the Buddha's core teachings are clearly and compellingly declared, their compassionate mediation calls for a complexity of which, as I have been suggesting, art is the best analogue.

THE DISCOURSES: LANGUAGE AS ART

Even in translation, the rhetorical sophistication of the Discourses is not difficult to detect. They are frequently ironic and satirical, shot through with elements of burlesque, and they deploy an effective variety of metaphors, parables, and narrative devices. For instance, in the *Ambattha Sutta*,[43] the Buddha deals with a young man, Ambattha, who is learned in the Vedas and is a pupil of the Brahmin Pokkharasati. Ambattha visits the Buddha to question him, but is arrogant and loud-mouthed, and the Buddha wonders if Ambattha would behave so rudely if he were talking to a Brahmin. Ambattha replies that he would not: "But as for those shaven little ascetics, menials, black scourings from Brahma's foot, with them it is fitting to speak just as I do with the Reverend Gotama" (113). This gratuitous insult is followed by an even more "angry and displeased" outburst, as Ambattha turns on the Buddha "with curses and insults," calling him into disrepute because of his Sakyan origins: "the Sakyans are fierce, rough-spoken, touchy and violent. Being of menial origin, being menials, they do not honour, respect, esteem, revere or pay homage to Brahmins" (113).

The Buddha now has had enough, and decides to deal with these puerile insults by playing Ambattha at his own game. He begins by setting out the standard classification of the four main castes, and proclaims that Ambattha is descended from a slave girl of the Sakyans. The astonished Ambattha does not know what to say, but the Buddha pursues him relentlessly: "If you don't answer, or evade the issue, if you keep silent or go away, your head will split into seven pieces" (115). The Buddha then repeats the threat, at which point Vajirapani the yakkha (ogre or demon) appears, "holding a huge iron club, flaming, ablaze and glowing, up in the sky just above Ambattha" (116). The unfortunate Ambattha sees the yakkha and is terrified, at which point the other young men who have been observing the exchange turn against Ambattha and shout violent insults at him. By and by, the Buddha relents: "It is too much," he says, "I must get him out of this" (116), which he does by telling a parable to demonstrate that caste is unimportant for attaining enlightenment.

Ambattha returns to his teacher, the Brahmin Pokkharasati, who is furious when he learns that the Buddha has been insulted: "You're a fine little scholar," says the Brahmin, and he became "so angry and enraged that he kicked Ambattha over" (123). Pokkharasati then decides to visit the Buddha to make amends, and the Buddha offers Pokkharasati a "graduated discourse" because his "mind was ready" (124). And so Pokkharasati hears the *Dhamma* and becomes a lay disciple.

Rhetorical contrasts are strongly marked throughout this energetic Discourse, as the Buddha responds vigorously to the insulting Ambattha, and then offers a "graduated discourse" to the better-disposed Pokkharasati. In both cases, the Buddha's language is geared to the mentality of his interlocutors, and in response to the young man, the Buddha engages in some comically burlesque exaggeration, culminating in the theatrical business of the yakkha, which upstages Ambattha by reversing the scare tactics that Ambattha himself had initially deployed. The Buddha's control of the entire staged performance is evident when he realizes that Ambattha needs rescuing, at which point the Buddha turns the conversation toward an explicit statement of principle, pointing out that caste, like Ambattha' s book learning, is not relevant to enlightenment. Clearly, Ambattha needs to be engaged differently from Pokkharasati, and the Buddha rises to the occasion, managing the arrogant and juvenile Ambattha with verve and tough humor. On the one hand, a key principle is affirmed (enlightenment does not depend on caste, lineage, kin-group, and the like); on the other, the Buddha engages effectively and imaginatively with the world's imperfections.

Similar rhetorical strategies occur throughout the Discourses, and should be read as integral to the Buddha's discernment of how best to engage with a variety of interlocutors who labor in different ways under the weight of their illusions and ignorance. For instance, in the *Kevaddha Sutta*[44] an inquisitive *bhikkhu* wonders how the four elements might "cease without remainder" (177). The *bhikkhu* visits the gods and asks the Great Brahma, who replies with some self-inflating bravado before taking the *bhikkhu* aside and quietly telling him he doesn't know the answer. Brahma then (also quietly) tells the *bhikkhu* that it was incorrect not to listen to the Buddha in the first place (179). The contrast between Brahma's public declamation and his privately delivered aside is amusing, and reveals also that his self-aggrandizement is a bluff—a smoke screen covering up his ignorance and incapacity to deal with the question. Although initially the *bhikkhu* sought in the wrong direction, he is brought at last to a new understanding of the Buddha's teaching on the "cessation of consciousness" (180), and the process of his learning is expressed in an engaging way.

A further example is provided by the *Kakacupama Sutta*,[45] which is about being patient, especially when someone is speaking offensively or disagreeably. The Buddha is concerned that people often harbor anger, even if they don't show it. To illustrate the point, he tells the story of a woman, Vedehika, who has a reputation for being even-tempered. Her maid, Kali, decides to test Vedehika to discover if anger "is actually present in her" (219). The maid provokes Vedehika so relentlessly that, at last, Vedehika strikes her with a rolling pin, after which Kali runs about displaying her wounded head and loudly proclaiming "the gentle lady's work" (220). The moral is quietly and clearly stated:

> So too, bhikkhus, some bhikkhu is extremely kind, extremely gentle, extremely peaceful, so long as disagreeable courses of speech do not touch him. But it is when disagreeable courses of speech touch him that it can be understood whether the bhikkhu is really kind, gentle, and peaceful. (220)

The slapstick aspect of the rolling-pin story stands in contrast to the straightforward conclusion that the Buddha draws from it, and the point is that monks who harbor unacknowledged anger are apt to behave no better than the irked housewife chasing her maid with a rolling pin. Yet this straightforward lesson gains significantly from its interrelationship with the slapstick anecdote, because the tale of Vedehika and the maid engages the reader in a moment of carnivalesque liberation from the strict guidelines of formal instruction. Even the most patient of us might feel some sympathy for the put-upon Vedehika, and in so doing we might also realize afresh how actual experience is more complex than the precepts by which we would regulate it.

Throughout the Discourses, imagination is frequently deployed to remind us how prone human beings are to irrationalities, phobias, and prejudices. Charnel ground meditations and extreme ascetic practices are favourite motifs by means of which the Buddha explores such disconcerting aspects of human experience.

For instance, in the *Mahasihanada Sutta*,[46] the Buddha advises the ascetic Kassapa, who recommends various extreme mortifications that are a testament, mainly, to how grotesque human behavior can be. Likewise, charnel ground meditations typically force us to dwell on the foulness of corpses and on the disgusting aspects of decaying human bodies. In both cases, the effectiveness of the writing depends on an initial, shocked recoil away from the unpleasant things imagination brings vividly to life; the wisdom of "not clinging to anything in the world"[47] will then be understood all the more feelingly.

The Buddha's evocation of such fearful aspects of our condition merges readily with frequent reminders of how consistently disappointing and threatening a place the world is. For instance, the *Mahadukkhakkhanda Sutta*[48] contains a charnel ground meditation connected to a meditation on the inevitable fate of a beautiful, well-born girl. The *bhikkhus* are asked to think of the girl's beauty, and then to imagine her as a corpse "in a charnel ground, one, two, or three days dead, bloated, livid and oozing matter" (183). But before they imagine this delectable sight, they are asked to think of the girl as an old woman, and then as gravely ill, "lying fouled in her own excrement and urine, lifted up by some and set down by others. What do you think, bhikkhus? Has her former beauty and loveliness vanished and the danger become evident?" (183). Here, charnel house and disease combine, and the Buddha's rhetorical shock tactics are all too obvious, as he aims to discourage indulgence in sensual pleasures, which, he argues, are a main cause of quarrels, armed conflict, and violence in general. Because pleasure is gratified by possession, people often quarrel to gain or retain property so that they can further indulge themselves. For this reason also, people commit violent crime, and, in turn, the state uses violence against the wrongdoers: "Again, with sensual pleasures as the cause . . . men break into houses, plunder wealth, commit burglary, ambush highways, seduce others' wives, and when they are caught, kings have many kinds of torture inflicted on them" (182). A catalogue of such tortures is provided, and it is monstrous, once more exemplifying the fearful but all-too-typical depravity of humankind.

In these examples, imagination is deployed to dissuade us from foolish attachments to transitory pleasures, which in turn are a source of suffering. Yet we might also notice a further dimension to the repeated meditations on death and disease. These meditations do not just cause us to recoil in horror; they also familiarize us with unpleasant facts that, for the most part, we prefer to ignore. Frequently repeated, vividly imagined evocations of sickness, disease, and death do indeed contain a warning about the futility of sensual indulgence, but also they offer an invitation to embrace even these facts of our human condition with equanimity. A *bhikkhu* should feel at home among the corpses, unafraid because fear itself is part of the suffering from which he seeks liberation. Likewise, the world-hating ferocity of the extreme ascetics is a manifestation of fear and loathing, and imagination helps us to understand that such behavior is harmful. After all, the meditation on the beautiful girl would not be effective if we did not appreciate and value beauty, just as we appreciate and value life and health. As always, the middle way requires discernment, and we need to be educated not only to understand the principle, but also to negotiate the felt complexities of our emotional lives, shaped as they are by forces, cultural and otherwise, beyond our conscious control.

So far, I have noticed how frequently the Discourses draw attention to language, and how there is a real analogy between a life conducted according to the *Dhamma* and a conversation that promotes understanding and insight. As we see, craving, desire, and attachment need to be convincingly, even sympathetically evoked if the unenlightened are to be instructed effectively about them. And so the Discourses teach us the high art of the detached agonist, the liberated one who nonetheless engages with the sufferings of others out of compassion, whose detachment is not indifference, and whose engagement is not indulgence.

In the *Lohicca Sutta*,[49] the Brahmin Lohicca makes a case for complete detachment and argues against attempting to share good doctrine, "for what can one man do for another? It is just as if a man, having cut through an old fetter, were to make a new one" (181). But the Buddha objects, and poses a question. If Lohicca were able to enjoy the entire "fruits and revenues" (182) of the region in which he lived, would this be a good thing, or would it be better for him to share these fruits and revenues and to consider the welfare of his tenants? Lohicca agrees that it would be better to share, and the Buddha applies the lesson to sharing the *Dhamma* in order to help those who are at various stages of the path toward release. In short, we are engaged with one another by the very nature of our being in the world, and it is wrong to act as if this were not so. Lohicca at last admits that the Buddha's teaching has been effective: "it is as if a man were to seize someone by the hair who had stumbled and was falling into a pit" (185). This comparison suggests that the Buddha's insight has been something of a desperate measure to save Lohicca from the consequences of misguided thinking. But the note of alarm and relief in Lohicca's statement suggests also that his new realization is not just intellectual, but carries an emotional charge. Again, the process of instruction entails the interdependence of reason and imagination, abstract precept and telling example. Let us now consider briefly a Discourse in which the Buddha's rhetorical self-consciousness is deployed to illuminate the key but difficult question of what happens to us after death.

In the *Potthapada Sutta*,[50] the Buddha visits the ascetic Potthapada, who is engaged in a noisy debate with his companions, "all shouting and making a great commotion" (159). Potthapada asks for quiet as the Buddha approaches, so that Potthapada can talk to the Buddha about "the higher extinction of consciousness" (160). In response, the Buddha provides an extended explanation of the levels of consciousness, progressing through the four *jhanas* and several further levels, until cessation is achieved (163). Potthapada responds by asking three questions: first, whether or not the soul is the same as the body; second, whether or not the Tathagata exists after death; third, whether or not the world is eternal. These are the familiar "undeclared points" that the Buddha typically refuses to answer, and when Potthapada asks, "why has the Lord not declared these things," the Buddha offers his standard reply: "Potthapada, that is not conducive to the purpose, not conducive to Dhamma, not the way to embark on the holy life; it does not lead to disenchantment, to dispassion, to cessation, to calm, to higher knowledge, to enlightenment, to Nibbana" (164). Potthapada wants to know what, then, exactly does the Lord declare, and the Buddha tells him: "Potthapada, I have declared: 'This is suffering, this is the origin of suffering, this is the cessation of suffering, and this is the path leading to the cessation of suffering" (164). These are the Four Noble Truths, stated clearly because they are conducive to a "holy life" (165), just as the undeclared points remain unanswered because they are not conducive to that end.

The Buddha departs, and Potthapada's fellow ascetics jeer at Potthapada, reproaching him for capitulating so readily to the Buddha's arguments. For their part, they say, they didn't "understand a word of the ascetic Gotama's whole discourse'" (165), and Potthapada admits that, well, he didn't understand either, but nonetheless he is convinced that the Buddha teaches the *Dhamma*, which is "a true and real way of practice" (165).

A few days later, Potthapada, accompanied by Citta, the son of an elephant trainer, visits the Buddha, who repeats his reasons for not answering the undeclared points. By contrast, he says, the Four Noble Truths are "certain" (165) because they lead to *nibbana*, and, not surprisingly, the old question of a substantial self is raised again, and this time the Buddha resorts to parables to make his point. If a man were to say, "I am going to seek out and love the most beautiful girl in the country" (166), his friends might well ask where she lives, what caste she belongs to, what is her name, clan, complexion, and so on. Wouldn't it be foolish to seek the most beautiful girl without having any idea about these practical matters? So it is with the soul's condition after death, in which "ascetics and Brahmins" (166) say they believe. In fact, they have no evidence for the soul's survival, or any idea how to achieve such a thing. A further similitude confirms the point. Suppose a man were to build a staircase for a palace without having any idea of the architecture of the building as a whole. Wouldn't that be foolish (167)? Just so, ascetics and Brahmins prescribe practices without having any real notion of what they are trying to achieve.

The Buddha then considers several ways in which an illusory sense of self might be acquired, and to assist his argument he turns to an analogy: "from the cow we get milk, from the milk curds, from the curds butter, from the butter ghee, and from the ghee cream of ghee" (169). Just so, the ways in which we describe the self resemble these ways of naming what we get from the cow, but, the Buddha insists, "these are merely names, expressions, turns of speech, designations in common use in the world, which the Tathagata uses without misapprehending them" (169). This is enough for Potthapada and Citta, both of whom now accept the Buddha's teaching. Potthapada asks to be a lay follower; Citta asks for ordination, and in a short time becomes an *arahant* (170).

As this brief summary indicates, the *Potthapada Sutta* is preoccupied with language, and, at the opening, Potthapada's companions are engaged in a noisy exchange of empty chatter, implicitly criticized by the burlesque humor with which it is described:

> There Potthapada was sitting with his crowd of wanderers, all shouting and making a great commotion, indulging in various kinds of unedifying conversation, such as about kings, robbers, ministers, armies, dangers, wars, food, drink, clothes, beds, garlands, perfumes, relatives, carriages, villages, towns and cities, countries, women, heroes, street- and well-gossip, talk of the departed, desultory chat, speculations about land and sea, talk of being and non-being. (159)

This list of assorted topics, combining the trivial and serious with equal haste and without distinction, suggests in a mildly humorous way that empty vessels do indeed make most noise. The fact that the group becomes quiet as the Buddha approaches confirms how unedifying this chatter is in his eyes. Then, as if to right the balance, Potthapada engages the Buddha in the metaphysical conversation about a "higher extinction of consciousness" (160). Yet even this radical shift in the tone of the conversation is not without irony because the metaphysical language itself turns out to be more idle chatter, despite its apparent elevation.

When Potthapada's companions turn on him with a barrage of insulting language (they "reproached, sneered and jeered at Potthapada from all sides" [165]), they show how little progress they have made and how little they have understood. By contrast, the Buddha sets out his main precepts clearly; he tells us they are "certain" (165), and, combined with a holy life, they lead to "disenchantment, to dispassion, to cessation" (164). Here, the Buddha stresses disengagement, in contrast to the chatter and clamor of Potthapada's friends. Instead, the Buddha speaks impersonally, calmly, and clearly, explaining his main teachings through a series of formulaic repetitions. Yet the fact remains that this recommended disengagement is not adequately understood by the ascetics or by Potthapada himself, and their subsequent unruly verbal exchange represents and confirms their incomprehension. In this context, the Buddha shifts his own discourse to engage his interlocutors more fruitfully by deploying a set of carefully chosen and developed parables and analogies. The first (the story of the most beautiful girl in the country) focuses on desire, and the second (the staircase) focuses on understanding. In both cases, the Buddha deals imaginatively with wrongheaded views about the self in ways that an unenlightened person can grasp. Although he emphasizes that the path to liberation requires "detachment," he insists also on maintaining "a true but subtle perception" (161) and, as we see, his teaching combines both elements. Self-reflexiveness about language is a central element in this Discourse as a whole, as different kinds of conversation, learned exchange, parable, analogy, irony, and dialogue are deployed to engage effectively with an unenlightened audience. Good timing, tact, and psychological insight reflect the Buddha's acknowledgment that values cannot be enforced, but are best presented by combining clarity and complexity. The position of the detached agonist is maintained here through the art of human discourse, and whether or not one believes in rebirth and *nibbana*, this vision of what it means to be human remains liberating and enabling.

REGRESSIVE INVERSION AND MISREADING

As I have argued, participation precedes analysis. That is, the circumstances of our nurture, such as language, family, and the mores of clan, caste, and nation, provide a matrix within which basic enculturation takes place through our largely uncritical belonging within the group. Individual autonomy develops with the capacity for independent thinking, but the freedom of an enquiring critical mind cannot simply be separated from the enculturated, bodily-rooted knowledge and affective life that is its prior ground.

With this in mind, I have suggested that Vedic tradition is a main nurturing source for Buddhism, providing a rich symbolism and ritual practice against which the Buddha's transcendent message defines itself, especially through a radical, disjunctive approach to language. Yet the Pali Canon everywhere acknowledges the centrality to Buddhism of dialogue with its own Vedic antecedents, and this dialogue is typically conducted in richly imaginative ways. As the Buddha well knows, too much emphasis on the conjunctive (as reflected in the requirements and assumptions of traditional observance, group morality, and the like) readily becomes tyrannical, superstitious, and intolerant. Similarly, too much emphasis on the disjunctive (through a thoroughgoing transcendence of attachments) leads to solipsistic isolation and a chilly, scarcely human detachment.

The art of the Discourses confirms the importance of finding a middle way between these opposites as the best means of promoting compassionate understanding, a prerequisite of enlightenment. Yet conducting a dialogue between the affective and abstract, metaphorical and conceptual, conjunctive and disjunctive, traditional language and independent criticism, group identity and individual autonomy, is difficult and exacting. Nonetheless, the Discourses especially insist on how central such a dialogue is to the promulgation of an authentic and vital Buddhism, and I will want to argue that failure to understand this dimension of the Buddha's teaching leads to misapprehensions that can have disastrous consequences.

The points I have made in these opening chapters allow me now, in conclusion, to return to the idea of regressive inversion, a central mechanism by which such disastrous misapprehensions occur. As I have suggested, regressive inversion comes about when boundless aspirations to an unconditioned freedom (a consequence, as we see, of the Buddha's universalizing vision) are re-deployed to supercharge the passions associated with group loyalty. This process is *regressive* insofar as it reaffirms an exclusionary group identity, the very thing that the universal vision was designed to transcend. Also, it entails an *inversion* of value in so far as it draws power from the languages of transcendence, infused as these are by aspirations to an absolute, unconditioned liberty. As an attentive reading of the Discourses shows, the Buddha sought assiduously to avoid these all-too seductive and dangerous misreadings, and he does so by an implicit understanding that imagination can be a powerful moral agent. In the next section, I will consider the part played by regressive inversion in the writings of key Buddhist figures who deal with relationships between Buddhism and politics in modern Sri Lanka, and for whom the moral agency of imagination is, by and large, less persuasive and less salutary than in the Buddha's Discourses.

PART II

READING SRI LANKA

CHAPTER 3

SRI LANKA

BUDDHIST SELF-REPRESENTATION AND THE GENESIS OF THE MODERN CONFLICT

In the previous chapters I have drawn attention to the rhetorical complexity of the Buddha's teachings insofar as these are communicated discursively. As we see, the Buddha's dialogical method in the Discourses conveys his core teachings to people insufficiently prepared to understand them. By such means the Buddha is able to teach a transcendent, selfless universalism while remaining compassionately engaged with others in an imperfect world.

In this second section, my main topic is actual Buddhist practice in Sri Lanka during the Buddhist revival preceding independence from Britain in 1948, and then, subsequently, in Sri Lanka's descent into violent ethnic conflict, continuing until the present. My focus is confined to some aspects of political rhetoric, and I am interested mainly in three key figures who address relationships between Buddhism and politics. These are Anagarika Dharmapala (who spearheaded the Buddhist revival prior to independence), Walpola Rahula (who wrote during the independence struggle) and J. R. Jayewardene (president during the worst violence in the post-independence period). To prepare the way for a discussion of the writings of these figures, I want first to provide a brief assessment of Sri Lanka's ancient Buddhist chronicle tradition, which is widely acknowledged as having profoundly influenced twentieth-century Sinhala Buddhist self-understanding, and which offers some significant rereadings of the Pali Canon. These rereadings have stayed surprisingly alive in modern Sri Lanka, not least in the work of the three authors I have chosen to discuss in chapters 4–6. My argument therefore is conducted through a series of steps, each contributing to an understanding of the next. Just as we need to know something about the Vedas to grasp the rhetorical complexity of the Pali Canon, so our assessment of the Pali Canon enables us to understand how significant

45

are the rereadings offered by Sri Lanka's ancient chronicles, which in turn affect the self-understanding of modern Sinhala Buddhists.

THE CHRONICLE TRADITION

The most famous ancient chronicle is the *Mahavamsa*, which means "Great Genealogy" (though "*vamsa*" has a range of implications, including, for instance, tradition, legend, family, caste and custom).[1] Extensions of the *Mahavamsa* are sometimes known as the *Culavamsa* ("Lesser Genealogy"), to signify their subordinate position to the first chronicle, which was compiled by a *bhikkhu* named Mahanama in the sixth century (C.E.).[2] This distinction between greater and lesser is not deployed consistently, however, and some prefer to call the whole set of chronicles (which have been extended five times, down to and including the twentieth century), the *Mahavamsa*.

The sixth-century (C.E.) *Mahavamsa* draws on materials recorded in an earlier chronicle, the *Dipavamsa* ("Island Genealogy"), written in the fourth century (C.E.). The exact indebtedness of the *Mahavamsa* to the *Dipavamsa*, and to a further background of oral tradition on which the *Dipavamsa* draws, is disputed, but the *Mahavamsa* clearly takes up and develops an ancient legendary account of the arrival of Buddhism in Sri Lanka and its protection by Sri Lanka's monarchs. Indeed, Mahanama's main purpose in compiling the chronicle is to consolidate the relationship between the *Sangha* and the monarchy. The *Mahavamsa* thus is a court document, a declaration and celebration of the relationship between the monarchy and the *bhikkhus*.

The legendary origins[3] of Sinhala civilization are traced in the *Mahavamsa* to the mythical figure of Vijaya, who is said to have arrived in Sri Lanka on the day of the Buddha's *paranibbana* (his death or final realization of *nibbana*). Vijaya was descended from a Northern Indian princess who was abducted by a lion, and Vijaya's father was the result of their union. The word for lion, *sinha*, remains in the proper name, Sinhala—the people of the lion.

When Vijaya's father, Sinhabahu, came of age he fled, taking his mother and sister with him. The enraged lion gave pursuit and eventually was killed by Sinhabahu, who then married his sister, by whom he fathered sixteen sets of twin sons. Vijaya, the eldest, grew up to be delinquent, and was sent into exile. He took ship with seven hundred companions, and fetched up on the shores of Sri Lanka, ruled at that time by a queen named Kuvanna.

At first, Kuvanna attacked Vijaya, but then fell in love with him. He became her consort, and they had two children. But Vijaya grew tired of Kuvanna and sent for a princess bride from Southern India, from where his followers also sought wives. Kuvanna was banished, and her children (a son and daughter) sought refuge in the mountains of the central highlands, where they reproduced, founding their own lineage.

The violent and lurid aspects of this curious story have much in common with foundation myths and legends of other ancient cultures, but it is not difficult to detect the presence of certain motifs and concerns that remain relevant to modern Sri Lanka. For instance, the fact that Vijaya's origins are in Northern India was important to those in the late nineteenth and early twentieth centuries who argued for the distinctness of the (Aryan) Sinhalas, and their differences from Sri Lanka's (Dravidian) Tamils. Likewise, the unfortunate demise of Queen Kuvanna and her children's subsequent procreation in the remote central highlands is a way of explaining the origin of the Veddahs, an aboriginal people still inhabiting the island in small numbers. Also, the *Mahavamsa* tells us that the Buddha himself visited Sri Lanka three times, using levitation to get there. Vijaya's arrival in Sri Lanka is therefore auspicious because it lays the ground for the Buddha's special mission to the Sinhalas. Elsewhere, the *Mahavamsa* tells us that Buddhism was brought to Sri Lanka in the third century (B.C.E.) by Mahinda, son of the great Buddhist emperor, Asoka. Mahinda introduced the reigning monarch, Devanampiya Tissa (250–c. 207 B.C.E.) to Buddhism, and the king subsequently established the Mahavihara, the great Sri Lankan monastic center. Devanampiya Tissa also received important relics from Asoka (the Buddha's right collarbone and his alms bowl), and Asoka's daughter brought a branch of the sacred Bo tree under which the Buddha was enlightened.

The *Mahavamsa* does not expand upon the relationship between the Buddha's actual visits to Sri Lanka and the fact the Mahinda is said to introduce Buddhism at a considerably later date. Also, there is no evidence outside the *Mahavamsa* for the existence of Mahinda, but the important lesson imparted by the story lies in the acceptance by Devanampiya Tissa, not only of Buddhism, but also of the Asokan tradition of the righteous ruler who promotes and protects the *Sangha*.

The *Mahavamsa* recounts the reigns of sixty-one monarchs, ending with Mahasena. Most are treated summarily, with the exception of Devanampiya Tissa and, especially, Dutthagamini. A third king who receives special attention is Parakramabahu I, and in all three cases the *Mahavamsa* praises these monarchs for their success in unifying the people and protecting the *Sangha*.

The geographical center of Sri Lanka from approximately 200 B.C.E. to 993 C.E. was Anuradhapura. The people of the Anuradhapura period produced art and architecture of great sophistication, and constructed impressively engineered reservoirs (tanks), canals, and irrigation systems. The combination of temple, tank, and rice field has come to symbolize the basic structure of this remarkable culture, which in modern times has frequently been looked back upon with nostalgia.

Yet, as the *Mahavamsa* tells us, the monarchy at Anuradhapura was not free from conflict. Tamil kings occupied the throne at the beginning of the second century B.C.E., and the best known of these is Elara, who ruled for forty-four years until challenged by Dutthagamini. The campaign against Elara is described at some length in the *Mahavamsa*, and it is clear that Dutthagamini does not move against Elara because the Tamil king was unjust, cruel, or tyrannical. The *Mahavamsa* points out that Elara was a good ruler, and, when he is killed, Dutthagamini has him cremated honorably, and erects a monument in his memory.[4]

In constructing the "Dutthagamini epic" as he does, Mahanama wants to make clear that the heroic task in hand is not the defeat of injustice but the restoration of Buddhism. The overthrow of the Tamil king is required first and foremost because Sri Lanka cannot be united unless the monarch is Buddhist. Yet the story of Dutthagamini's triumphs (he defeats not just Elara but also thirty-two other Tamil leaders) makes uncomfortable reading, especially if we are to consider it a vindication of the core values of Buddhism.

For instance, in a well-known passage, Dutthagamini fastens a relic of the Buddha to his spear before he marches to war (170). Also, he asks for help from the *Sangha*, and is provided with five hundred *bhikkhus* who take the field with him (170). The war is a full-on spectacular, with flying red-hot iron, molten pitch, charging elephants, and sacked cities. "Kandula, the best of elephants" (173) bears Dutthagamini, and the final reckoning between Dutthagamini and Elara is preceded by a suspense-filled pursuit until at last Elara falls to Dutthagamini's spear. Meanwhile, carnage and mayhem have built to a luxuriant excess as "the water in the tank there was dyed red with the blood of the slain" (175).

After further battles, Dutthagamini "ruled over Lanka in single sovereignty" (175). But the luridness of Dutthagamini's battles might well cause a reader to wonder whether this is an appropriate kind of writing for a *bhikkhu* to engage in, and then, also, whether or not the war can be justified or condoned when assessed by the Buddhist principles of nonviolence and compassion. And so we meet Dutthagamini again after his final triumph, as he retires to his palace. There, on a perfumed terrace adorned with "fragrant lamps," and "magnificent with nymphs in the guise of dancing-girls" (177), he has nothing to do but relax into an indulgence of the senses, invitingly described in counterpoint to the graphically repellent depiction of the war. But Mahanama's point is that Dutthagamini "knew no joy" (177) because his conscience preys on him: "How shall there be any comfort for me, O venerable sirs, since by me was caused the slaughter of a great host numbering millions?" (178). A good question, though whether or not it pertains more to Dutthagamini's conscience than to Mahanama's is a moot point. Anyhow, "eight arahants" are sent to offer comfort and advice to Dutthagamini. What they say has (understandably) exerted a considerable fascination upon commentators:

> From this deed rises no hindrance in thy way to heaven. Only one and
> a half human beings have been slain here by thee, O lord of men. The

one had come unto the (three) refuges, the other had taken on himself the five precepts. Unbelievers and men of evil life were the rest, not more to be esteemed than beasts. But as for thee, thou wilt bring glory to the doctrine of the Buddha in manifold ways; therefore, cast away care from thy heart, O ruler of men! (178)

That is, Dutthagamini can rest easy because there was only one committed Buddhist and one halfhearted Buddhist among the enemy troops; the rest were to be considered not human at all, "not more to be esteemed than beasts." The main point is the honor Dutthagamini brings "to the doctrine of the Buddha," and this greater good justifies the violence required to bring it about. Consequently, the juxtaposition of "doctrine of the Buddha" and "ruler of men" is central to the passage, as Mahanama (yet again) seeks to affirm that the righteous ruler is, above all, the protector of Buddhism.

The passage makes uneasy reading, and in his interviews with modern *bhikkhus*, Richard Gombrich found they were by and large disconcerted and would not have been inclined to think about the problem posed by this part of the Dutthagamini epic had he not pressed them. Although there was some variation in the answers Gombrich received from the *bhikkhus*, the "general tenor" of their response was that "Dutugamunu's killing of Tamils was sin, but not great, because his main purpose (paramartha) was not to kill men but to save Buddhism."[5] Although the *bhikkhus* disagreed about exactly how culpable Dutthagamini was in causing wholesale death and destruction, they by and large maintained that the end justified the means.

Without a lot of further reflection, modern activist *bhikkhus* who found themselves caught up in Sri Lanka's violent conflict could (and did) look just as uncritically to Dutthagamini as an example to imitate. Indeed, the *Mahavamsa*'s principal hero was widely regarded as exemplary by proponents of twentieth-century Sinhala nationalism along a wide variety of fronts. Thus, in the 1980s, journalists talked about "the *Mahavamsa* mentality,"[6] referring, broadly, to the heroic defense of Buddhism and the unification of Sri Lanka expressed by the Dutthagamini epic, which was energetically revived in support of modern Sinhala nationalism. Certainly, the three main figures with whom I am concerned in the following chapters seek deliberately to cast themselves in Dutthagamini's mold. Anagarika Dharmapala saw Duttagamini as a rescuer of Buddhism and the nation; Walpola Rahula condones Dutthagamini's resort to violence and recommends more of the same; J. R. Jayewardene not only compared his own achievements to those of Dutthagamini, but suggested also that in some respects he had done rather better than his legendary forebear. As Steven Kemper points out, "Sinhala politicians" find Dutthagamini "wherever they look,"[7] and various civil groups and political movements have declared themselves inspired by the heroics of the ancient king.

Although, as we shall see, the *Mahavamsa* does not have a modern concept of a nation-state, it insists on a special link between Buddhism in Sri Lanka and the Sinhalas, descendants of Vijaya. It also condones violence in defense of that special relationship. Admittedly, the civil conflict in modern Sri Lanka does not result just from an interpretation of texts, but it is nonetheless fuelled by the idea of a historical mission that such texts impart. And so the ghost of Dutthagamini has lived on, reclothed in modern dress—and now also equipped with modern weapons.

Among the many monarchs whose reigns are recorded in the *Mahavamsa*, Dutthagamini remains the most important, but two others (in addition to the founder, Vijaya) also are singled out. These are Devanampiya Tissa, who welcomed Mahinda's delegation from Asoka, thereby establishing Buddhism on the island, and Parakramabahu I, who ruled in the twelfth century (C.E.), after Polonnaruva had become the central city, rather than Anuradhapura.[8] Like Dutthagamini, Parakramabahu I fought wars and reformed and unified the *Sangha*. But as with Mahanama's account of Dutthagamini, the compiler Dhammakitti (who wrote the account of Parakramabahu I in the first extension of the *Mahavamsa*)[9] does not dwell upon the king's militarism. Yet again, the compiler's main point is that the monarch unified the country and protected the *Sangha*.

Something of this uncomfortable accommodation of violence and institutional Buddhism is evident even in the *Mahavamsa*'s opening mythological account of the Buddha's fabled visits to Sri Lanka, where he subdued the inhabitants, the Yakkhas, so that his doctrine should eventually "shine in glory" (3). Initially, the Buddha hovers in the air above the Yakkhas and we are told that he "struck terror to their hearts" (3–4). He then afflicts them with "rain, storm, darkness and so forth," and again they are "terrified." At last, he settles them in "the pleasant Giridipa" (4) (the name derives from "giri," or highlands, to which the Yakkhas are banished).[10] As David Little correctly points out,[11] the earlier *Dipavamsa* differs from the *Mahavamsa* in stressing the Buddha's concern for the Yakkhas' happiness. For instance, in the *Dipavamsa*, the "compassionate, merciful great Sage" wants to "administer joy" and so he finds a "charming and delightful island" for the Yakkhas, who are "highly satisfied."[12] This solicitude is downplayed in the *Mahavamsa*, which offers a more strenuous Buddha, bent on clearing a way for the establishment of his teaching at a future date. The *Mahavamsa*'s account is thus in keeping with Mahanama's general message that the political unity of Sri Lanka under Buddhism requires the removal of uncooperative groups, and the Buddha himself shows that a bit of muscle might be required to effect such a removal. Vijaya, Dutthagamini, and Parakramabahu I confirm the general point, and, all in all, Mahanama's lesson for monarchs remains consistent: be as strong as you need to be to maintain the Buddhist state; be supportive of the *Sangha* and willing to defeat the enemy by force. The advice was not lost on Sri Lanka's modern Buddhist revivalists.

As Heinz Bechert[13] says, the key to modern Sinhala national identity lies in the linking of religion and the people in Sri Lanka's ancient chronicle tradition. As we see, according to the *Mahavamsa*, Sinhalas are specially chosen by the Buddha and their political unity guarantees the survival of Buddhism in Sri Lanka, just as their political identity is guaranteed by their espousal of Buddhism. Certainly, in the Buddhist revival that preceded and helped to bring about independence from Britain in 1948, this coalescing of people, religion, and land was immensely persuasive and powerful. Yet, the *Mahavamsa* does not map directly onto late-nineteenth and twentieth-century Sri Lanka, and the political conditions described by Mahanama are not those of a modern postcolonial nation attempting to practice democracy. This fact was often ignored by revivalists bent mainly on reasserting what they took to be a time-hallowed, divinely sanctioned Sinhala Buddhist identity, which they invoked as part of their resistance to colonialism. Consequently, modern rereadings of the *Mahavamsa* supplement the ancient chronicle's rereading of the Pali Canon. And so, by increments, the nets of regressive inversion have closed around the Buddha's exalted promise of a universal liberation, confining that remarkable vision increasingly within the precincts of a passionately asserted national and ethnic solidarity.

As we have seen, Vijaya and his men married Southern Indian women; consequently, Aryan and Dravidian were mingled in Sri Lanka from the start. Subsequent migrations from Southern India continued to diversify the population, as is evident partly from the names of castes (such as Karava, Salagama, and Durava) that are Indian in origin but were adopted by Sinhalas.[14] Also, the Veddahs were no doubt largely assimilated by the newly arrived settlers. But there is no concern in the *Mahavamsa* for anything like modern ideas of race or ethnicity, and, as Tambiah[15] points out, the polity as a whole comprised assorted, loosely affiliated groups frequently at war with one another (we recall that Dutthagamini conquered thirty-two leaders, and it seems that Tamils had some Buddhists on their side, just as Dutthagamini had some Tamils on his).[16] Until approximately the tenth century, Tamils might well be Buddhists, and the last Sri Lankan kings, the Nayakkars,[17] were Tamil, though they pretended to be Buddhist in public to preserve the appearance of traditional order.

Late nineteenth- and twentieth-century claims to a pure Sinhala identity invested with an innate right to rule a Buddhist Sri Lanka therefore ignore the actual hybridity of the population through its long evolution. They also ignore the fact that the *Mahavamsa* deals mainly with relationships between the *Sangha* and monarchy, unlike the modern reformers whose main focus is on the people,[18] defined by race, religion, language, and the land. For their part, the people knew the stories of the ancient heroes mostly without having read the *Mahavamsa*; the chronicles were, after all, written in Pali and preserved in monasteries. The actual complexity of the *Mahavamsa* would, in any case, have caused little surprise to many ordinary Sri Lankans who already experienced firsthand a complex diversity and mingling of cultural influences in their daily lives.

In a fascinating analysis of popular religion in Sri Lanka, Gombrich and Obeyesekere[19] show that although language and religion gave the Sinhalas "a distinct cultural identity," such "fundamental institutions as kinship are Dravidian in form, and so are many aspects of the traditional spirit religion" (134). Hindu deities such as Kataragama, Kali, and Huniyam are frequently taken over and legitimated as Buddhist, together with such extravagant, originally non-Buddhist practices as fire-walking, extreme body-piercing (for instance, hanging from hooks), drumming, and ecstatic dancing. As a typical example of this kind of syncretism, Gombrich and Obeyesekere cite a legal dispute in which Tamils contested the use of a Hindu shrine by Sinhalas. The presiding Sinhala judge was visited in a dream by the Hindu god Kataragama, who told him to decide in favor of the Buddhists, which he did (187). Again, a Sinhala governor of the Central Bank facing criminal charges sought the protection of the Hindu deity Huniyam by crawling around a shrine on all fours (35), and "practically every politician" pays homage to the god Skanda "in order to win an election or ensure the national electoral success of the party" (185). In short, Hindu deities have been eclectically adopted by many Buddhists, and especially among alienated urban workers and villagers for whom traditional kinship structures were weakened as a consequence of mid-nineteenth-century laws affecting the sale of land. Unprecedented levels of social mobility meant that traditional bonds supporting group identity were replaced by a new enthusiasm for the magical invocation of deities whose propitiation would lead not only to the protection of one's self and one's family, but also the affliction of one's enemies (129–30). An urgent need therefore persists in popular Buddhism for a strongly conjunctive language and for practices confirming people's intimate ties to one another; the manner in which popular Buddhism draws on Hindu devotional practices answers this need. But in a modern Sri Lanka bent on achieving independence from Britain, the sense of belonging and of loyalty to a group is supplied also by a fast-growing enthusiasm for the idea of a Sinhala national identity, and here an interesting, highly significant interpretive exercise comes into play, which can be summarized as follows.

The Buddhist revival was closely bound up with the idea that the return of a pure Buddhism and of a true Sinhala identity would occur together. The revivalists held that colonialism had corrupted the Sinhalas, making them torpid and servile while also causing Buddhism to become ineffectual and superstitious. For the revivalists, the popular Buddhist enthusiasm for Hindu devotions was an embarrassment—sad evidence of how superstition had sullied the Buddha's message and reduced the Sinhalas to indolence. All such practices must now be discontinued, so that the Buddha's pure teaching can be heard.

In one sense, this is a conservative argument, foregrounding the austere, disjunctive aspect of the Buddha's core teachings, while expressing impatience with the conjunctive attachments, loyalties, and need for group identity supplied by what is held to be superstitious practice. But the revivalists then take a further step, ironically at odds with their own main argument against popular practice. They do so by maintaining that the revival of a pure Buddhism will further Sri Lankan nationalism. That is, the sense of belonging to a group is now supplied by the conviction that the Sinhalas have an inherited right to prevail in Sri Lanka. Thus, modern ethnic nationalism reconfigures the popular need for belonging, but remains unaware of the degree to which it in fact replaces one idol with another. As I have mentioned, the revivalists also maintained that resistance to colonial rule and the restoration of a Buddhist polity along the lines set out in the *Mahavamsa* would be accomplished together. With this in mind, let me now turn briefly to Sri Lanka's colonial history.[20]

COLONIZERS, MISSIONARIES, AND THE BUDDHIST REVIVAL

The great civilizations centered first in Anuradhapura and subsequently in Polonnaruva endured until approximately the end of the thirteenth century. Polannaruva was abandoned for reasons that remain unclear, perhaps having to do with the spread of malaria and the intensive labor required to maintain dry-zone irrigation. But everything changed in Sri Lanka with the arrival in 1505 of the Portuguese, the first of the three main colonizing powers who occupied the island until 1948.

The Portuguese were concerned to exploit Sri Lanka's wealth and strategic advantage, and also to convert the inhabitants to Christianity. Missionaries sought to suppress Buddhism, and their methods of conversion were as persuasive and coercive as they thought necessary to encourage compliance. However, in 1658, the Portuguese were ousted by the Dutch, who made an alliance with the King of Kandy. But the Dutch presented such a huge bill for their labor that the King found himself indentured, and soon realized that his supposed liberators had not so much defeated the Portuguese as replaced them.

Dutch anti-Catholicism was more vigorous than Dutch opposition to Buddhism, and rooting out the hated religion of the Portuguese became a matter of some urgency, not least because Catholic ceremonialism had proved more effective for missionary purposes than Calvinist iconoclasm.[21] Still, Christian missionary activities continued to be coercive, and, for instance, laws were passed to prevent the inheritance of land by non-Christians. Meanwhile, the Dutch East India Company went on extracting maximum profits from the spice trade, much as the Portuguese had done.

Eventually, the Dutch were replaced by the British, who occupied Sri Lanka from 1796 to 1948. Again, Kandy looked to the British for aid against the Dutch, but as the Kandyans might have expected, the British East India Company behaved much as the Dutch East India Company had done, and hostilities soon broke out between the British and the disgruntled Kandyans. Things came to a head in 1815, when rebellion was quelled and the resultant Kandyan Convention granted sovereignty of the island to Britain. In turn, the British agreed to protect Buddhism by acknowledging "the religion of the Boodhoo professed by the chiefs and inhabitants of these provinces," and by promising to support "its rights, ministers, and places of worship."[22]

This official British toleration of Buddhism helped to provide political stability whereby the spice trade could flourish. Cinnamon remained especially profitable, but in the early nineteenth century the British introduced coffee to the island, and developed a plantation system. This new enterprise was so successful that, to maximize its potential, Buddhist temple lands were taken over, causing resentment among the dispossessed. Also, a Tamil labor force was brought from South India to work the plantations. At the beginning of the twentieth century, these "Indian Tamils" or "Estate Tamils" numbered some 500,000, constituting roughly twelve percent of the population. They considered themselves (and in turn were considered) distinct from Sri Lankan Tamils, and their immiseration was, and remains, a serious political issue.

Toward the end of the nineteenth century, tea replaced coffee as the main plantation crop. Unlike coffee, tea could be harvested throughout the year, and the climate was ideal for producing a high-quality leaf. This, together with rubber (another new crop), proved highly profitable. Yet the intensive cultivation of crops for export at the expense of subsistence crops led to widespread rural poverty and fuelled an indignation against colonialism that would declare itself especially vigorously in the twentieth century.

A further source of indignation against the colonizers arose in the aftermath of the Kandyan Convention (1815), when the British discovered that protecting Buddhism according to traditional expectations required the appointment of monastic officials, administration of property, upkeep of shrines, and so on. The main opposition to the government's providing such services came from Christian missionaries, mainly Anglican and Methodist, who campaigned for the advancement of Christianity and the extirpation of Buddhism, which was condemned as idolatrous.

The redoubtable Wesleyan missionary, R. Spence Hardy, writing in 1841, exemplifies the case made by the missionaries in general against government policy. Hardy's tellingly entitled, *The British Government and Idolatry in Ceylon*,[23] begins by assuring readers that "Britain is now the first of the nations in wealth, and power," and the reason is "that we might carry on with better effect the great work of the world's conversion" (6). The British empire preeminently spreads "the flame of Christian benevolence," stirring up the spirits of "good men" (7) everywhere in support of the true religion. Hardy pauses briefly to notice that the aforementioned Christian benevolence entails "the entire destruction of the empire of hell" (7), within which he locates "the national religion of Ceylon," namely "Budhism [sic]" (9). Because "The religion of Budha [sic] is idolatrous," and because nothing is more clearly condemned in the Bible than idolatry, the "necessity" (9) of destroying Buddhism is evident.

Hardy's next step is to accuse the British government of aiding and abetting idolatry, thereby furthering the interests of the "empire of hell" (7). He supplies lists (16 ff) of temple services, tax remissions for temple lands, and stipends for "Buddhist priests," all supported by the government. He goes on to assure us that the governor, Sir Robert Brownrigg, is beyond reproach in his "respect for revelation"; rather, the Kandyan Convention itself was either "very improperly worded" or "it was blasphemy" (37). The unctuously aggressive suggestion here is that the respectfully Christian Brownrigg would more likely be mistaken than blasphemous, and now that he has been shown his error (stupidity, not heresy), he, and the government he represents, will mend their ways.

As Hardy moves toward a conclusion, he roundly affirms his own faith in the colonial enterprise: "I speak advisedly," he says, "that no land ever shone upon by an eastern sun had greater reason to rejoice in its Government, than the people of Ceylon in the beneficent aspect of the British rule" (45). Moreover, we should know that "the natives at large see their privilege, and are grateful for the boon" (46).

The insufferable Hardy is not yet done, however, and becomes more insufferable still when he pauses to notice the part played by military conquest in the colonial enterprise he so admires. He assures us that English soldiers ("brave men" with "blood-stained swords") want only to placate the natives who would then be "awakened from their stupor" (46) and rush to the service of Christ. In short, military victory is condoned because it accelerates "the destruction" of Buddhist idolatry, so that "the blessings of the Truth" may be "diffused" instead (8).

Hardy expresses a typical missionary attitude to Buddhism,[24] and I have considered his arguments mainly to show how the Buddhist revivalists had much to be grieved about. Christian missionary aggression, the exploitation of natural resources, and the expropriation of land were immensely damaging to the island's colonized inhabitants. Meanwhile, the promised government protection of Buddhism came to nothing, but dwindled (at best) into a policy of noninterference, as the missionaries got down to their work of extirpating "idolatry" and replacing supposed Buddhist superstition with "the blessings of the Truth" in the form of Christianity. And so, for the majority Sinhala population, colonial exploitation and contempt for Buddhism had become inextricable, and a Buddhist revival was, understandably, part and parcel of the anticolonial agenda.

Nonetheless, the Buddhist revival did not simply stand opposed to Christian missionary activity; rather, it deployed techniques of argument, organization, and propaganda learned directly from the missionaries. This interesting phenomenon has led Gananath Obeysekere to coin the term "Protestant Buddhism,"[25] and to provide some context for Obeysekere's much-discussed description, it is helpful to consider the effects of colonial education, especially the missionary schools.

Although Hardy parted company with the government on the Kandyan Convention, he and the government were of one mind in promoting Western education through the English language. In 1869, the government opened a Department of Public Instruction to supplement and promote the English-medium education already established by the missionaries.[26] Although traditional monastic education did not die out (indeed, it gradually strengthened in the later nineteenth century), Sinhala-medium schools could not compete with Western curricula that provided access to political advancement and the broader world of modern science and technology. Consequently, as Gombrich and Obeysekere say, "it remained the case till well after Independence that education at an English-medium school was the sole point of entry to the ruling elite."[27] Leach concludes that "by the second decade of this century the whole of the Ceylonese middle and upper classes had been very thoroughly Anglicised," and, commenting on this statement, Bond notices that it is difficult to be sure about the "exact extent of Westernization," but "clearly the English-educated elite, who came to occupy influential positions in society, became very Westernized."[28]

Although traditional monastic schools survived, the educational role of the *Sangha* was much diminished, and the *bhikkhus* lost contact with the new mainly urban, English-educated elite.[29] Yet this educated elite by and large did not lose contact with Buddhism, even though adopting Western ways and receiving an English education that included instruction in Christianity. As Gombrich and Obeyesekere point out, "the influence of Christianity was rarely more than skin-deep," and "despite the best efforts of the missionaries, only a minority even of the pupils at mission schools became Christians."[30] One result was an increasing demand among English-educated laypeople for a modern, accessible, and intellectually coherent Buddhism. Partly in response, and in reaction also against the relentless colonial-missionary denigration of Buddhism, a revival took shape in the later part of the nineteenth century, reflecting, as we now see, criteria and expectations imparted by the colonizers' own educational practices.

Not surprisingly, in this context, the Buddhist revival adopted Christian missionary techniques for self-promotion. Thus, *bhikkhus* acquired printing presses to publicize their teachings, and agreed to defend Buddhism in open debate against the Christian missionary challenge.[31] A series of debates took place at Baddegama (1865), Varagoda (1865), Udanvita (1866), Gampola (1871), and Panadura (1873). The most famous is the final one, at Panadura (near Colombo), where, before an audience estimated at some 5,000 to 7,000 people, the powerful Buddhist orator, Mohottivate Gunananda, debated the Rev. David de Silva, a Wesleyan clergyman, in a two-day exchange at the end of which Gunananda "carried the multitude with him,"[32] though both sides (of course) claimed victory.

In the same year as the Panadura debate (1873), the Vidyodaya Pirivena (Buddhist monastic college) was founded, to be followed in 1875 by the foundation of the Vidyalankara Pirivena. These colleges admitted lay students as well as *bhikkhus*, and were influential in promoting the Buddhist revival. The Vidyalankara Pirivena especially was a seedbed for the nurturing of activist *bhikkhus* whose "*Mahavamsa* mentality" led them to engage directly in political protest, the most extreme example being the assassination by a *bhikkhu* of the prime minister, S. W. R. D. Bandaranaike, in 1959. In a later chapter, we shall look more closely at Walpola Rahula, an internationally famous Buddhist scholar and teacher at the Vidyalankara Pirivena, and a key figure in developing a rationale for the political *bhikkhus*.

In addition to these initiatives, the Buddhist revival gave rise to various groups and societies modeled on Christian organizations. Examples are the Society for the Propagation of Buddhism (modeled on the Society for the Gospel) and the Young Men's Buddhist Association.[33] The Buddhist Theosophical Society merits special notice here, not only because of its importance in helping to revive Buddhist education, but, again, because of its Western origins. The Theosophical Society was founded in the United States in 1875 by Madame Helena Blavatsky and Colonel Henry Steel Olcott, a former Union officer in the American Civil War. When Olcott and Blavatsky read about the Panadura debate, they visited Sri Lanka, arriving in 1880, intent on supporting the Buddhist cause. Olcott especially encouraged Buddhists to develop their own education system, and he founded the Buddhist Theosophical Society. Later, he developed a Buddhist Theosophical School system, which was very successful. It is also worth noticing that Mohottivate Gunananda introduced to Olcott and Blavatsky a young protégé, the sixteen-year-old Don David Hewavitharne, later to become famous as Anagarika Dharmapala.

By coining the label "Protestant Buddhism," Obeyesekere attempts to describe some main characteristics of the complex reform movement that I have now briefly outlined. Yet there are some obvious differences between the Protestant Reformation in Europe and the Sri Lankan Buddhist revival. For instance, unlike European Protestants, Sri Lankan Buddhist laypeople had little access to scriptures in Sinhala, and Buddhists by and large maintained respect for the *bhikkhus* and the *Sangha*, unlike European Protestants who repudiated monkhood and the institutional Roman Catholic Church. But the strong emphasis on lay participation and the development of meditation (hitherto reserved for the virtuosi *bhikkhus*)[34] among laypeople were remarkable innovations analogous to the European Reformation. Also, revivalist *bhikkhus* readily adopted the Christian missionaries' preaching style,[35] exhorting people to moral virtue, social engagement, industriousness, sobriety, and punctuality—in short, to virtuous behaviour appropriate for the daily activities of laypeople interested in getting ahead in a modern industrialized world. Thus, Anagarika Dharmapala drew up a detailed code of conduct consisting of two hundred rules for the guidance of laypeople, pertaining to such matters as dress, eating, cleanliness, and the like.[36] He also insisted that a true Buddhism should reject as superstitious many popular devotional observances, including drumming, fire-walking, and various kinds of magic. Such things were corruptions of Buddhism, and Obeyesekere's parallel to the Protestant Reformation is helpful here, insofar as it draws attention to a new, lay moral emphasis and to a repudiation of superstition in the interests of a purer form of observance, which, in turn, was seen to promote the Sinhala national cause.

However, despite denunciations delivered in the name of a pure Buddhism, popular religious practices did not die out. Indeed, they increased, and it is likely that to some degree the idealizing moral insistence of the revivalists precipitated a carnivalesque return of the repressed. Certainly, traditional and modernist types of Buddhism coexisted, often with complex crossovers.[37] Also, as I have suggested, annexing the Buddha's universalism to the common human need for belonging within a group occurred in analogous ways in both popular Sri Lankan observance and among the reformers who promoted nationalism. Yet the reformers were not inclined to see the analogy. They thought of themselves as recovering an ideal that had been realized in the Anuradhapura period, and they scolded the popular traditionalists for being backward. Yet they were less unlike the popular traditionalists than they thought. Today, commentators by and large agree that the revivalists were pretty much inventing the national ideal rather than recovering it, and, as we have seen, there is no sense in the *Mahavamsa* of anything like the Sinhala national or ethnic identity widely proclaimed by the Buddhist revival as central to good government in post-Independence Sri Lanka. As Gunawardena points out, the word "Sinhala" in ancient Sri Lanka was used in several senses—for instance, to indicate a religious affirmation, a spoken language, or status according to caste.[38] Also, the polity in ancient times was made up of a loose aggregate of settlements under a central authority in a "multicentric and dispersive array,"[39] as Tambiah says:

> The effective political arena extends beyond any single "kingdom"; it is multicentric, with rival "kingdoms" jostling each other, changing their margins, expanding and contracting, according to the fortunes of wars, skirmishes, raids, and diplomacy. They were pulsating galactic polities. (173)

People from many backgrounds lived within these "multicentric polities," but were not identified as "ethnic 'Sinhalese' or 'Tamils' as they are conceived today."[40] In short, although discussion continues about the exact constitution of the ancient Sri Lankan political order, there is a consensus among scholars that modern nationalist rereadings of the *Mahavamsa*, identifying the Sinhala as a distinct ethnic group marked by religion, language, and land, are substantially a modern invention. Also, there is broad scholarly agreement about the part played by modern European theories about race in the construction of such an identity.

Theories about racial difference, and the superiority of some races over others, developed in the late nineteenth century in the West. In part, these theories grew out of linguistic studies pertaining to the idea of an Indo-European family of languages, to which Max Muller attached the term "Aryan."[41] This term soon was taken to describe not only the language but also the people who spoke it, and, drawing on these ideas, Western colonizers found it convenient to be convinced of their supposedly innate superiority over those to whom they were dedicated to bring enlightenment. Certainly, the British did not hesitate to impose racial categories on the inhabitants of Sri Lanka, as is clear in the 1871 census that required people to identify themselves in such a manner.[42]

Remarkably, theories about racial difference brought to Sri Lanka by Westerners were eagerly seized upon also by some proponents of the Buddhist revival. By demonstrating that the Sinhala language was Indo-European, Western scholars allowed the Sinhalas to conclude that they too were Aryan—that is, Northern Indian as distinct (especially) from the Dravidian or Southern Indian Tamils. Drawing on such ideas, theorists of the new Buddhism were better able to imagine an ancient Aryan Sinhala race, united by language and ruling over a righteous Buddhist Sri Lanka. Reformers influenced by such thinking were able easily to read back an idealized view of Sinhala racial identity into the ancient chronicles, and they did so to help make their case for their own right to govern.[43] Three books written close to independence (1948) are often cited as central to the ideology and assumptions of this aspect of the Buddhist revival. These are Walpola Rahula, *The Heritage of the Bhikkhu* (1946), D. C. Vijayawardhana, *The Revolt in the Temple* (1953), and the report by the Buddhist Commission of Enquiry, *The Betrayal of Buddhism* (1956). All three define Sinhala nationalism consistently in terms of race, religion, and land. I will deal later with Rahula; for now, a brief look at *The Revolt in the Temple*[44] will clarify the main point.

The full title is *Dharma-Vijaya (Triumph of Righteousness) or The Revolt in the Temple*, and a further version is provided on the following page: *The Revolt in the Temple. Composed to Commemorate 2500 Years of the Land, the Race and the Faith*. The first title suggests that revolt is in the interests of spiritual liberation (the "Triumph of Righteousness"), whereas the second suggests that it is in the interests of a particular group defined by land, race, and faith. As Vijayawardhana's argument develops, it becomes clear—often disturbingly so—that he sees these two broad concerns as inseparable, and he holds fast to the idea that the Buddhist Sinhalas are ordained from ancient times to govern the island.

Interestingly, Vijayawardhana proposes a modern socialist Buddhism in which the excessive impersonality of Marxism and the excessive pursuit of individual perfection in traditional Buddhism can learn sufficiently from one another to enable the development of a politically effective Buddhist state:

> The *thesis* of traditional Buddhism and the *antithesis* of Marxian Communism are incomplete. They contain both merits and defects. The Buddhist tends to regard the perfecting of the individual as the essential task of religion, and thus to ignore the need for constructing a better order of society: the Communist tends to assume that a change of system is sufficient and that the conversion of the individual is irrelevant. . . . The Buddhist is so entangled in the chains of tradition that he is a stranger in the world of current politics: the revolutionary is so impatient towards traditional claims that he ignores the values contained in the past order, and is accordingly crude in his criticisms of religion and apt to disregard the cultural assets of religion. (603–4)

This passage provides some sense of how readily activist *bhikkhus* could be attracted to revolutionary socialism. Indeed, the influence of Marx on a wide range of ideas and practices in Sri Lankan politics in the postindependence period is considerable. Yet, in citing this passage, I am mainly interested in how central Buddhism remains to Vijayawardhana's vision of a new Sri Lanka. Thus, in a preface, we are assured that Vijaya is "the founder of the Sinhalese race" (3), and the *Mahavamsa* is cited to back up the claim. Also, with "the Buddha's blessing" there is an "intimate connection of the Land, the Race and the Buddhist Faith" (4), and in writing the story of "the Sinhalese race," the author offers to put us back in touch with a "forgotten world" (5). In a foreword, Pahamune Sri Sumangala rehearses the same broad set of ideas, focusing on "Two thousand five hundred years of Buddhism, of the Sinhalese race, and of civilization in Lanka" (15), and Vijayawardhana argues that "the birth of the Sinhalese race" was "a pre-destined event of high import and purpose. The nation seemed designed, as it were" to be the custodian of Buddhism, the bearer of "the Torch that was lit by the great World Mentor twenty-five centuries ago" (32). The "World Mentor" (the Buddha), is "the fairest flower of that mighty tree of the great Aryan race" that "has held the moral and intellectual supremacy of the world" (33). Vijawardhana goes on to provide a highly idealized view of the ancient Aryans, describing them as having "a supreme ardour and zest for living," as being without "inhibitions" and with "no sense of fear and dread in the subconscious mind" (34). Above all, he wants to restore this gloriously unspoiled quality of life to Sri Lanka, according to the terms set out by the *bhikkhus* who composed the Kelaniya Declaration of Independence in 1947, proclaiming the right to "a Free and Independent Sovereign State" (158). Mainly, colonialism is blamed for having corrupted the Aryan people and their culture, which can be restored by the simultaneous revival of true Buddhist doctrine and the expulsion of the colonial overlords. Here, as elsewhere among the ideologues of the revival, Buddhism clearly serves the interests of a group defined in terms of race and nation, and whose aims are unapologetically hegemonic. As we see, this is quite contrary to what the Buddha himself taught; indeed, it is a danger the Buddha is at pains to warn against, and it is also what I mean by "regressive inversion."

POLITICS AND CONFLICT

The history of Sri Lanka's independence movement and its aftermath is extensively documented[45] and I want, briefly to notice only a small number of key political events to supplement the previous description of some central aspects of the Buddhist revival and its links to Sinhala nationalism.

The British prepared the way for independence by drafting the Donoughmore Constitution in 1931 and the Soulbury Constitution in 1947. Donoughmore proposed that government of Sri Lanka should be by executive committee, elected by universal suffrage. Minorities, especially Tamils, worried that this arrangement favored the Sinhalas, and that there were insufficient protections for minorities within Sri Lanka's diverse population (including not only the special interests of Sinhalas and Tamils, but also of Muslims, Veddahs, Christians, and Burghers). Complaints lodged especially by Tamils and Muslims were partly addressed by Soulbury in 1947 as part of the final push to independence in 1948. Yet, although some adjustments were made, Soulbury still recommended majority rule and rejected a Bill of Rights. In light of subsequent events, Lord Soulbury himself later expressed regret that his commission did not provide better protection for Sri Lanka's minority populations.[46]

The handover of authority in 1948 went smoothly and the British-educated elite, both Sinhala and Tamil, took over the business of government, sharing an expertise based on their common knowledge of English. The first prime minister, Don Stephen Senanayake, envisioned a pluralist, secular society, and although he understood the political importance of publicly acknowledging his Buddhist heritage, he seriously misestimated the groundswell of Sinhala Buddhist nationalism that soon swept him from power.

The principal agent of this all-but irresistible new political force was S. W. R. D. Bandaranaike, who in 1936 founded a group called the Sinhala Maha Sabha (The Great Sinhala League) as a means of promoting the Buddhist nationalist cause. Bandaranaike was raised as an Anglican, but converted to Buddhism and was much influenced by Anagarika Dharmapala. In 1951, Bandaranaike split from the ruling United National Party (UNP) and formed the Sri Lanka Freedom Party (SLFP). He campaigned for policies reflecting the principles of the Buddhist revival, and he campaigned for Sinhala to be made the single official language.[47] In 1956, the year of the Buddha Jayanti, Bandaranaike's SLFP achieved an overwhelming electoral victory confirming, among other things, the political influence of the Buddhist revival. Certainly, activist *bhikkhus* were strongly supportive of the SLFP, and many campaigned on Bandaranaike's behalf.

Tamils were understandably alarmed at these developments, and, for his part, Bandaranaike rapidly became critical of the utopianism of the political *bhikkhus* and their nostalgia for an ideal, ancient Sinhala way of life. Also, he came to see that some Tamil grievances were well founded, and he entered into negotiations with the Tamil leader, S. J. V. Chelvanayagam. The result was the Bandaranaike-Chelvanayagam Pact (1957). This important agreement accorded "national language" status to Tamil, and made provision for the main Tamil area of Sri Lanka, namely, the northern and eastern provinces, to be administered in the Tamil language. Also, a system of regional councils would provide a counterbalance to the power of an otherwise highly centralized government.

The Bandaranaike-Chelvanayagam Pact offered a power-sharing approach to government as a way of averting conflict, and although the pact itself was abandoned, it sets out the main elements of the only kind of settlement likely to succeed in the long run. There is an interesting parallel in the Sunningdale Agreement of 1973, devised to resolve violent ethnic conflict in Northern Ireland. Although the Sunningdale Agreement was also abandoned, its main ideas were revived some twenty-five years later in the Good Friday Agreement of 1998, as the basis of a complexly organized power-sharing executive. The Good Friday Agreement has had its troubles, but remains the most feasible approach to Northern Ireland's all-but intractable problems, and the parallels with Sri Lanka are striking.

Predictably, however, Bandaranaike's attempts to reach an agreement with the Tamils met with resistance from the Sinhala nationalists who had helped Bandaranike get elected (including the political *bhikkhus*, who now became especially hostile). In the upshot, the pact failed to win support, and a major outbreak of violence occurred in 1958,[48] followed by a series of riots (for instance, in 1977, 1981, 1983) that catapulted Sri Lanka into the spotlight as one of the world's most dangerous conflict zones. In 1959, Bandaranaike was assassinated by a *bhikkhu*, putatively for not having fulfilled his promises to establish a new Sinhala Buddhist state.

Not long after her husband's death, and following a brief change of government, Bandaranaike's widow, Sirimavo, became prime minister in 1960.

Eventually, in 1970, she formed the coalition United Front (UF) to oppose the UNP in the upcoming election. She was successful, and in 1972 her United Front government declared Sri Lanka a republic. A new constitution was drafted, and to the further dismay of the Tamil minority it accorded Buddhism "the foremost place" in a state that would "protect and foster it"; also, Sinhala was declared the official language, with the use of Tamil permissible by statute. The government also undertook a controversial university admissions policy aimed at curbing the disproportionately large number of Tamils enrolled in higher education. The question of university admissions is complex, but the resentment produced by the new legislation, especially among young Tamils, was deeply felt and immediate.

In response to rising tensions, an ultra-left nationalist group, Janatha Vimukthi Peramuna (JVP; People's Liberation Front), emerged in 1971. The JVP comprised mostly young Sinhalas who were prepared to offer violent opposition to any government attempts at conciliation with Tamils, who, for their part, began seriously to consider a separate Tamil state. The Tamil United Liberation Front (TULF) was formed to promote the separatist agenda that was formally declared in 1976; meanwhile, mirroring the revolutionary violence of the JVP, the Tamil underground produced its own paramilitary organizations, the best-known of which is the Liberation Tigers of Tamil Eelam (LTTE), founded in 1976 by Velupilai Prabhakaran.[49] The stage was now set for an escalation of violence that has, to date, cost approximately 66,000 lives.[50]

In 1977, the UNP under the leadership of J. R. Jayewardene defeated Sirimavo Bandaranaike, winning an overwhelming 140 of 168 seats. Jayewardene's decisive victory was in large part attributable to the economic woes brought upon Sri Lanka by the previous administration's socialist economic policies. Jayewardene was a proponent of free enterprise and industrialization, but, like S. W. R. D. Bandaranaike, he was also a devout Buddhist. He even campaigned for what he called a *dharmistha* society—that is, a righteous society modeled on his admired Asoka, the third century B.C.E. Indian ruler whose government supported and promoted Buddhism. Yet Jayewardene insisted on keeping the *bhikkhus* out of politics; they were to set an example for the government but should not themselves engage in political action. Nonetheless, he lavishly supported Buddhist culture, and his government dedicated large sums of money to the preservation and repair of Buddhist artifacts and to updating the *Mahavamsa* to cover the period from 1935 to 1977.

In a controversial move, Jayewardene called for a new constitution (1978) to replace the Westminster system of government with a French-style presidency. He argued that a presidential system would provide much-needed stability, enabling the country's pressing problems to be addressed more effectively. Jayewardene also declared Tamil a "national language" and changed the controversial university admissions policy. All in all, he sought to redress some of the imbalances that developed under the Bandaranaikes, but too much momentum had already gathered, both among Tamil separatists and Sinhalese chauvinists, and his conciliatory efforts were by and large unsuccessful. In face of increasing Tamil violence, Jayewardene found himself constrained to introduce a Prevention of Terrorism Act (1979), and he himself was a target of the JVP, which made a nearly successful attempt on his life.

Serious disturbances occurred in 1977 and 1981, but the worst riots took place in 1983 and were directed against Tamils, especially in Colombo. Perhaps a thousand people died, and many thousands fled to refugee camps. Security forces abetted the anti-Tamil mobs, and there was a breakdown of law and order for almost a week. By and by, the government took strong measures to counter the powerful Tamil backlash, eventually sending troops to occupy the Jaffna peninsula, the main Tamil stronghold in the north. At this point, India threatened military action in support of the Tamils, and Jayewardene was forced to make concessions. He negotiated with Indian Prime Minister Rajiv Gandhi and, on July 29, 1987, the Indo-Sri Lankan Agreement was signed.

The agreement called for the Northern and Eastern Provinces of Sri Lanka to be combined for administrative purposes and to be granted increased autonomy. Because of the large population of Muslims and Sinhalas in the Eastern Province, a referendum should be conducted to determine whether or not that Province wished to remain joined to the Northern Province. There should also be an immediate ceasefire, and the Indian Army would undertake to guarantee the decommissioning of Tamil weapons.

All too predictably, the Indian Peacekeeping Force (IPKF) soon ran into opposition from the LTTE, which had come out against the agreement, and efforts to quell the increasingly violent Tamil Tigers soon led the IPKF into outright war. Meanwhile, Sinhala resistance to the agreement also turned violent, as the JVP assassinated government officials (among others) who were deemed to be supporting a policy that would partition Sri Lanka. In 1986, a group of radical *bhikkhus* founded the Mavbina Surakime Vyaparaya (MSV), the Movement for Protecting the Motherland, and found common cause with the JVP in fighting to maintain the geographical unity of Sri Lanka so highly valued by the Buddhist reformers.

Jayewardene retired in 1988, and was succeeded as president by Ramasinge Premadasa. Initially, the JVP favored Premadasa because he opposed the agreement, and when he became president, he released JVP prisoners in a conciliatory gesture. Premadasa then successfully negotiated the withdrawal of the IPKF (they finally left in 1990), but by and by he was forced to confront the JVP, against whom he mounted an extremely violent and effective campaign, virtually disabling them, not least by killing Rohana Wijeweera, the JVP's founder-leader. In 1989, Premadasa himself was assassinated by a suicide bomber, and the Tamil Tigers are thought to be responsible. In 1991, Rajiv Gandhi was also assassinated, and in 2006 the Tamil Tigers virtually admitted responsibility.[51]

Since the beginning of the twenty-first century, governments in Sri Lanka have continued to address the dire issues that I have now briefly described. Most notably, in 2002, a ceasefire was successfully mediated by Norway, and seemed to promise a breakthrough. But at the time of writing, hostilities have resumed, and between July and early August 2006, some eight hundred people were killed in Sri Lanka—almost exactly the same number as in the Israel-Lebanon war in that same period.[52]

This brief outline of some main events in Sri Lanka's recent political history provides a context for the three authors I will discuss in the following chapters: Anagarika Dharmapala, Walpola Ralula, and J. R. Jayewardene, all of whom were pious Buddhists. Rahula was a *bhikkhu* and Jayewardene a layman; Dharmapala spanned both categories, living the life of an ascetic (Anagarika) apart from laypeople, yet without being ordained—though in the last year of his life he did become a *bhikkhu*. My focus is not mainly on the biographies and political careers of these three, but on how their writings reveal their complex and sometimes contradictory involvement in the Sinhala nationalist cause, which, as we see, has been linked to Buddhism throughout Sri Lanka's recent history. I will be concerned with how, as devout Buddhists addressing the nationalist debate, these three figures are caught up also in the seductively dangerous inversion of value that occurs when a universal religious vision entailing selfless, unconditional commitment is re-deployed to supercharge the passions confirming group loyalty and identity. By contrast, the Tamil cause, it should be noted, is mainly separatist and not closely linked to religion.

In short, in the writings of Dharmapala, Rahula, and Jayewardene we will see something of the elusive processes whereby undiscerned prejudice can override principle despite good intentions. The means by which misreadings are produced, identities imagined, and various kinds of violence instigated, even from within the framework of a genuine commitment to religious values, are my main concern in the following chapters. By contrast, as the Buddha recommends (and countless devoted Buddhists demonstrate in their daily lives),[53] a discerning critical compassion combining detachment and engagement, disjunctive self-consciousness and conjunctive accessibility, might show us the way at least toward some mitigation of the egregious harm that we continue to find reasons to inflict on one another.

CHAPTER 4

ANAGARIKA DHARMAPALA

BUDDHISM, SCIENCE, AND THE
CRISIS OF HISTORICAL IMAGINATION

The writings of the remarkable Anagarika Dharmapala bring together many key elements of the Buddhist revival and its links to the nationalist movement that I have now described. Thus, Dharmapala is a fierce opponent of colonialism, which he sees as having degraded the Sinhalas and reduced their religion to a futile set of ritual practices. He is convinced that a Buddhist revival would have a salutary influence on his fellow Sri Lankans and would awaken them from their colonial sleepwalking. He argues that Buddhism is preeminent among the world's religions because it transcends caste, kin, and race, while promoting its main, humanizing message of toleration and compassion. By contrast, he condemns the monotheistic religions for being exclusionist and violent. Hinduism is criticized for some of the same reasons, and, again, for its dependency on superstitious ritualism. Dharmapala also looks to the *Mahavamsa* to confirm the relationship between Buddhism and the special interest of the Sinhalas, whom he describes as racially distinct and whose historical destiny is to rule Sri Lanka.

But how could Dharmapala reconcile his high praise for Buddhist universalism with these ideas about a special Sinhala privilege? In the following pages I want to suggest that the answer lies partly in his enthusiasm for modern science as an agent of progress. For Dharmapala, science is objective and universal, and he was optimistic that it would join forces with a similarly objective and empirical Buddhism to restore a lost golden age to Sri Lanka. In opting for scientific clarity at the expense of the more subtle kinds of discernment that we have seen exemplified by the Buddha's own teaching practice, Dharmapala misestimated a powerful exclusionist element in his own thinking, which in fact prevented him from promoting the tolerance, compassion, and universalism which he admired. To understand more fully how such a state of affairs developed, let us briefly consider Dharmapala's life and writings.

THE MAKING OF A SUBVERSIVE

Don David Hewavitharne[1] (1864–1933), who later took the name Anagarika Dharmapala (Homeless Protector of the Dharma), was born into a wealthy Buddhist family in Colombo. His parents wanted their son to have what they considered to be the best modern education, and so they sent him to Christian schools. There, the young Don David was required to study the Bible, but his interest was not inspired by devotion; rather, he realized that a close knowledge of the Christian sacred scripture would enable him to attack Christianity itself all the more effectively. Throughout his life he remained a scathing critic, especially of the Old Testament (which he thought Christians should discard), and he has harsh things also to say about Jesus, for whom, however, he also had some qualified admiration.

By his own account, Don David was a thorn in the side of his teachers, and was threatened with expulsion from school if he did not desist from his negative criticisms of the Bible. Also, the young pupil was distressed by the insensitivity of many Western Christians with whom he came in contact, and, partly as a result, he discovered a new appreciation of Buddhism, the superiority of which seemed evident to him not least because it was held in such contempt by those entrusted with his formal education.

The indignation caused by his early schooling stayed with Anagarika Dharmapala throughout his life. An account in the *Spectator* (30 January 1926) describes an address given by the ailing sixty-one-year-old Darmapala in London. The chair informed the audience that the speaker was "most infirm" and would therefore remain seated. But when Dharmapala came to recount his early schooling, "he rose to the full six feet of him and brandished a walking stick at the audience. 'I learned your faith in a mission school in Ceylon,' he said, 'and one day the missionary took his gun and shot some little birds—so— and so! That made me revert to the faith of my fathers.'"[2] Presumably, Dharmapala brandished his walking stick to simulate the missionary at work with the gun ("so—and so"); also, the walking stick is pointed at the audience, on whom Dharmapala trains his aim, just as the missionary did with the birds. It is a belligerent bit of instruction, and the combative disposition it expresses is characteristic of Dharmapala's own "missionary" (his term)[3] endeavors on behalf of the Buddhist revival.

Not surprisingly, the young Don David found solace and inspiration in the example of the powerful Buddhist orator, Mohottivatte Gunananda,[4] who in turn recognized the young man's talent. But, as I have noticed in chapter 3, the series of Buddhist-Christian debates culminating in Gunananda's impressive performance at Panadura in 1873 had another result that also greatly influenced Don David's career. As the publicity accorded to the debates spread beyond Sri

Lanka, it attracted the attention of Colonel Henry Steel Olcott and Madame Helena Blavatsky, founders of the Theosophical Society. These two promptly dispatched themselves to Sri Lanka, where they set about helping to organize Buddhist resistance to Christianity, especially in education. Among other initiatives, Olcott produced his highly successful *Buddhist Catechism*, first published in 1881 and reissued in an expanded form in more than forty editions. It is still used in Sri Lankan schools today, and affords a remarkable example of how the Buddhist revival was able to draw on Christian methods of instruction—in this case, catechetical. Gunananda introduced Don David to Olcott and Blavatsky, who took the young man under their wing when he was sixteen years old, recognizing his unusual abilities. Don David then worked assiduously for the Buddhist Theosophical Society and changed his name, dedicating himself to the religious life as a homeless wanderer (Anagarika). He chose not to become a *bhikkhu*, though he accepted ordination shortly before he died.

On a visit to India in 1891, Dharmapala was upset to discover the derelict condition of the ancient temple at Buddhagaya, and promised to restore it. The following May, he founded the Maha Bodi Society, dedicated to the restoration of ancient Indian Buddhist sites and relics. Dharmapala's cause was rapidly internationalized, and brought him into contention with Hinduism, about which he developed a set of opinions every bit as caustic as his diatribes against the Old Testament.[5] Also, as a further consequence of his new interest, he broke with the Theosophists after a serious quarrel with Olcott about the authenticity of the Tooth Relic, and a growing concern that the Theosophists favored a syncretistic, liberal Hinduism at the expense of the singular truth claims of Buddhism.

Dharmapala's agenda as a champion of Buddhism was fundamentally shaped by these events of his early education and youthful experience. From his schooldays, he developed a poor opinion of Christianity, and especially of Christian missionaries and their colonizing countrymen. From Gunananda and his allies he learned the value of informed polemical discourse, using the enemy's weapons and techniques. From Olcott and Blavatsky, he learned the value of a practical Buddhism that could be taught catechetically and which appealed to an urban, Western-educated audience. This powerful mix of elements was further influenced by Dharmapala's own scholarly talents, irrepressible energy, and intense conviction. Consequently, as Bond says, Dharmapala became "the most influential individual in the Buddhist revival,"[6] and Seneviratne describes him as the "founder of Buddhist modernism," claiming also that "no major Sinhala thinker or writer after him has escaped his influence."[7] Yet, because Dharmapala spent a large portion of his life in India, he was less famous as a Sri Lankan national hero during his lifetime than after his death, when his legacy was better understood. Since then, as Guruge says, "the Anagarika's name has been a household word in every nook and corner of the Island."[8]

AGENDA FOR REFORM

As a polemicist and advocate for Buddhism, Dharmapala is frequently an exciting thinker and a compelling writer, yet his arguments remain so closely bound up with the cause of Sri Lankan nationalism and anticolonialism on the model I have described in chapter 3 that he is also frequently disconcerting. Basically, he asserts the right of the Sinhala "race" (as he frequently says) to rule the island of Sri Lanka, and he argues that the right of inheritance enjoyed by Sinhala "sons of the soil" is validated by Buddhism.[9]

For the most part, Dharmapala's writings are addressed to specific audiences and are designed to meet the requirements of particular occasions. He was fluent in Sinhala and English, and the substantial collection of his work edited by Ananda Guruge comprises letters, addresses, journal articles, pamphlets, occasional essays, and diary entries. Yet, despite these varied contents, a small number of themes reappear constantly, often supported by the same examples and quotations. Repeatedly, Dharmapala hammers away at the same central ideas, and once we grasp what these are, his writings hold few intellectual surprises, though they are often interestingly varied in ways that reflect his assessment of the needs and capacity of different audiences.

Dharmapala's main aim is the promotion of Buddhism, which he considers superior to other religions.[10] Thus, the Buddha is "the greatest [reformer] the world has ever seen" (351), and religions that do not teach the Noble Eightfold Path "are founded on Ignorance" (58). "False are alien faiths" (58), he tells us, and we should embrace "the religion of the Buddha" because it offers a uniquely "comprehensive system of ethics, and a transcendental metaphysics embracing a sublime psychology" (8). Moreover, Buddhism does not depend on "abstract principle," but is "realistic" and "free from all super-human agencies and devoid of all anthropomorphic conceptions" (351). It is a "spiritualized democracy" (78) and, repeatedly, Dharmapala draws attention to the fact that Buddhism transcends caste, as well as national and racial differences: "As Buddhism acknowledges no caste system, and admits the perfect equality of all men, it proclaims the universal brotherhood" (21). Toleration and compassion are identified as key virtues, in the practice of which, Dharmapala assures us, other religions—especially Hinduism, Judaism, Christianity, and Islam—are found seriously wanting.

Thus, for instance, Dharmapala maintains that monotheism gives rise to violence and vengefulness because monotheistic religions are tribal and maintain that God favors a particular group. Dharmapala holds firm to the conviction that "the founders of monotheistic religions have been invariably bloodthirsty, despotic, and cruel" (418), and he is unremitting in his condemnation of the religious views of Jews, Christians, and Muslims. Yet Vedic tradition fares no better, and is also denounced as tyrannical. Thus, Isvara is described as the "supreme of despots" whose priests are nothing better than "a selfish body of irrational swindlers" (192). The sacrifice ritual is likewise condemned (200, 204), and, in Dharmapala's opinion, narcissistic "worship of self" has led to "the complete degradation of the Hindus" (363).

In expressing such opinions, Dharmapala is keen to show how well Buddhism compares to the violence and "muddleheaded" (55) (a favorite epithet) confusions of the world's main religions. Frequently, the satire is deliberately extravagant, its amusing excess shot through with a scathing anger. This formidable mixture of elements can remind us that Dharmapala did not consider his task to be theoretical, but exigent.

In promoting Buddhism as a compassionate, universal religion free of ritualism and transcending the constraints of caste and kin group, Dharmapala demonstrates a clear understanding of the Buddha's teachings on these matters, but he adds his own distinctly modern observation by insisting that Buddhism is entirely in tune with the empirical views and attitudes of Western science. Repeatedly, he claims science (especially the theory of evolution) as the ally of Buddhism and the enemy of Christianity. "Buddhism is a scientific religion," we are assured, "in as much as it earnestly enjoins that nothing whatever be accepted on faith" (20). The universe was not "caused by the will of a foolish ignorant despotic phantom Creator," but is the result of an "unerring natural Immutable Law of Cause and Effect" proceeding by way of "gradual evolutionary development" (79). Also, science has "helped to destroy the power of the Christian church," and geology combined with "Darwinian evolutionism gave a shock to the pet theories of muddle-headed prelates," just as "the sledge hammer attacks of Huxley, Tyndall, Herbert Spencer, on Biblical fortifications were destructive and formidable" (405–6). Darwinian evolution is certainly a great deal "more acceptable to Buddhists than the Genesis theory" (435) because Buddhism, like science, is "progressive" (445). By contrast, Christianity "has been a complete failure in Europe" (452), and eventually "with its unscientific doctrines of creator, hell, soul, atonement, will be quite forgotten" (465).

These views of Buddhism as a "pure science" (658) as opposed to a fearmongering and superstitious Christianity are repeated with mantra-like persistence, and in this light Dharmapala is unsparingly harsh about such traditional Buddhist practices as astrology, ritual prayer, and other kinds of observance that he dismisses also as superstitious. Thus, he berates Sinhala villagers as "indolent, ignorant, illiterate" (721) and denounces the ill-educated *bhikkhus* (519) who mislead them. He even fears that the decay of Sinhala Buddhism is so far advanced that in another ten years it might "cease to exist" altogether on this "historic island" (521).

Predictably, Dharmapala identifies colonialism as the main culprit in bringing about the all but fatal decline and enervation of Sri Lankan Buddhism that he laments so energetically. "There is something about an alien rule" he tells us, "no matter how beneficent, that stupefies" (694), and, as with the struggle for home rule in Ireland, the path to an independent Sri Lanka and to a revitalized Buddhism will be difficult (533). But did not the colonizers also introduce Sri Lanka to modern education and modern science? Dharmapala neatly dodges this objection by insisting that the colonizers were not concerned about providing a scientific or technological education in their Sri Lankan schools, which were, instead, mainly instruments for Christian proselytizing. At his Church of England boarding school Dharmapala learned "very little history and arithmetic but pored over Bible lessons from morning till evening" (684), and, in general, "European science, European industries, European arts, ship building, engineering, building of bridges, railways, and experimental chemistry, and all the economic sciences that have helped to make the European races were not taught." Instead, the "freebooters who came to Asia to plunder and destroy ancient civilizations" were driven by "Mammon" and had no interest whatsoever in improving the "helpless peoples" (398) whose wealth they seized for export, without obligation or remorse. It follows that one way to undermine the Christian colonizers and their missionary henchmen would be for young Sinhalas to acquire a good scientific and technological education. For this reason, Dharmapala advises Sinhala youth to visit "the United States, Japan, Germany, India, Hongkong, France and England to learn technical sciences," and then return to work for the "national elevation" (512) of their country.

Still, Dharmapala did not turn his back entirely on ancient Sinhala Buddhist traditions; rather, he thought that a pure Buddhism prevailed in ancient Sri Lanka, and one main result of a revival would be the recovery of some aspects of what was lost. This is a final—and highly significant—element in the scheme of Dharmapala's thinking, and it gives rise to some special difficulties.

Dharmapala found evidence for the Buddhist golden age in "the most authoritative among all Asiatic histories" (691), namely, the *Mahavamsa*. But he takes the *Mahavamsa* always at face value, without questioning the point of view of the compilers or attempting to distinguish between myth, legend, and history. Rather, he is captivated by the idea that there was once throughout the island "a purely religious civilisation" (486), which he maintains will flower again when the colonizers depart. He is convinced that Sri Lanka has a special destiny, and that "Lanka, the pearl of the Indian Ocean, the resplendent jewel" was chosen to become "the future repository of the pure religion of the Tathagato" (481); moreover, the Sinhalas are "a unique race" (479), "a superior race" (515). Not even the simplest peasant can entirely forget his religion, because it is "in his blood" (540), and "to the Sinhalese without Buddhism death is preferable" (541). For Dharmapala, pure Sri Lankan Buddhism and the Sinhala "race" are everywhere synonymous, and in asserting this opinion he draws upon late-nineteenth-century European theories about racial characteristics, thinking that in so doing he is, once more, on the side of science. It is an easy step for him then to claim that through the fault of the British, "the Aryan Sinhalese has lost his true identity and become a hybrid" (494).

Dharmapala's compact between ethnicity, nationalism, and religion was to bear unexpected bitter fruit after independence, when his anticolonial arguments were re-deployed by those who continued to promote the Buddhist revival, directed now especially against Tamils who were seen, like the British, as presenting an impediment to a righteous society in which Buddhism was the state religion and Sinhala the official language. In this context, it is worth noticing that, however much occluded by the urgency of Dharmapala's anticolonial polemic, a certain exclusionist prejudice weaves a dark thread throughout his work. "The Muhammedans," we learn, are "an alien people" who "by Shylockian methods became prosperous like the Jews" (540), and, like the colonizers, Muslims thrive at the expense of "the Sinhalese, sons of the soil" (540). Muslims are "alien to the Sinhalese by religion, race and language," and, consequently, "there will always be bad blood" (541) between the two groups. And when Dharmapala denounces the "tribal god" of Horeb as cruel (405), it is all too easy to commute this denunciation of the god to the people primarily associated with him:

> To the historian of the Aryan race a knowledge of the five Nikayas is essential. Thousands of scholars are to be found in Europe, they study the history of the degenerate tribe of Israel and then they begin to spin cobwebs trying to catch into their nets, the undeveloped minds of the ignorant. (499)

The "Aryan race" here is Sinhala, and the link between "race" and religion ("Nikayas") is posited as "essential." We then pass to the European biblical scholars, described as studying a "degenerate tribe"—that is, another "race" which is, like the Sinhalas, identified by religion, except that in this case the religion, and the people associated with it, are bent mainly on entrapment as they "spin cobwebs" and deploy "nets." Again, religion is racialized, and religious differences are the markers of further "essential" differences among separate kinds of people.

When Dharmapala describes Christianity as the "bastard offshoot" (57) of Judaism, he reaffirms the significance of race by using the language of genetic transmission. But he is willing also to acknowledge some positive elements in Christianity, which, however, he attributes to the fact that Christianity "borrowed a large stock of ethics from Buddhism" (57). This is especially evident, he thinks, in the Sermon on the Mount (696), and based on the fact that Christians and Buddhists share a substantial body of core teachings, Dharmapala is able to call upon them to work together against colonialism and "for the elevation of the

Sinhalese people" (510). Still, this strategic anticolonial compact between Buddhism and Christianity in Sri Lanka would cease as soon as the "elevation of the
Sinhalese people" had been achieved and the "purely religious" (486) civilization
of the *Mahavamsa* restored. Dharmapala's ecumenical gesture is therefore more
apparent than real, as Christianity is called upon to cooperate in its own demise,
yielding to the superior claims of the religion from which it has derived its own
best teachings in any case.

The Vedas, the Hebrew scriptures and the New Testament loom large in
Dharmapala's writings; by contrast, Sri Lanka's Tamils are treated in a minor
key, partly because their concerns are subsumed under Dharmapala's assessment of Hinduism in general. The main exception is Dharmapala's account
of the exploits of the legendary King Dutthagamini in the *Mahavamsa*, and
especially Dutthagamini's defeat of the Tamil King Elara.

Dharmapala begins by characterizing the Tamils as "fiercely antagonistic
to Buddhism," and, in the Dutthagamini epic, Tamils committed acts of van-
dalism against sacred Buddhist shrines. But King Elara soon gets his comeup-
pance at the hands of the "wonderful prince," Dutthagamini, and Dharmapala
pauses to assure us that the war was of "a religious character." Duttagamini himself proclaims that it "had for its object the re-establishment of the religion of
the supreme Buddha"; consequently, he took with him into battle a group
of *bhikkhus*, "the sons of Buddha," and the wars were then "conducted in a spirit
of religion." Finally, we are reminded that, throughout the Dutthagamini
epic, religion is "completely identified with the racial individuality of the
people" (488–89).

When Dutthagamini suffers a pang of conscience because of the large
number of enemy dead, the *bhikkhus* reassure him, pointing out that the enemy
forces were almost entirely non-Buddhist, so that their extermination is not a
matter for regret. Dharmapala cites the passage (I have reproduced it in full in
chapter 3) unflinchingly, without reflecting on its disturbing aspects, which, indeed, he confirms by praising the Sinhalas' "racial individuality" for having contributed significantly to the outcome of the war.

Elsewhere, Dharmapala praises "our heroic and patriot king, the Righteous
Dutthagamini" (501), and notices that "for nearly one thousand one hundred
and seventy-six years the Sinhalese maintained their independence by the
strength of their arms" (503). With the same enthusiastic confidence, Dharmapala exhorts an audience of young Sinhala men to "Enter into the realms of our
King Dutugamunu in spirit and try to identify yourself with the thoughts of
that great king who rescued Buddhism and our nationalism from oblivion"
(510). The young men who are advised to follow Duttagamini's good example
are invited also to affirm the inseparability of race, religion, and nationalism,
and to accept that violence might be required to preserve an integral Sinhala
Buddhist Sri Lanka.

SCIENCE, IDEALISM, AND
CULTURAL NATIONALISM

The ideas I have now described are woven throughout Dharmapala's writings and remain consistent even as they are adapted to fit the needs of different audiences. As we see, the positions for which he argues are sometimes commendable, as in his assessment of the abusive aspects of colonialism. But we might wonder how he could recommend the Buddhist virtues of universal compassion and tolerance while also promoting an exclusionist, racially defined nationalism, to be defended if necessary by force of arms. As we see, Dharmapala himself acknowledges that Buddhism is designed to liberate people from the constraints of tribal and kin groupings, and yet he appeals to Sri Lanka's Buddhist history to promote an "ethnoreligious fundamentalist" agenda, as Eva K. Neumaier[11] says.

To explore this contradiction, I want briefly to return to Dharmapala's idealized view of Buddhism and of the precolonial conditions under which he says it flourished. Thus, he insists on "universal virtues" that require people to be treated with "perfect equality" (21), and which enable the development of a "brotherhood without distinction of caste and race" (19). He also acknowledges that Buddhism "strongly condemns war" (22), and he praises qualities such as "universal pity, kindness, and non-sectarian ethics" (215). Consequently, "the message that I bring to you is one of love, of purity and of self control." In brief, he offers "a simple re-echoing of the idealistic doctrine that was preached twenty five centuries ago" (352). Also, he reminds us that the Buddha placed "the strongest emphasis" (8) on the "supreme importance of having an unprejudiced mind" (8), and that "concord alone is meritorious" (17).

It is important to notice that Dharmapala did not think of these teachings only as ideals to which we might aspire. He thought that they had been realized already in ancient Sri Lanka, and he invites us to imagine the "pure, refined, kind-hearted children of Lanka" (482) in precolonial times. "A more joyous, contented race, it is impossible to imagine," he says, than these "Aryan Buddhists" who spread the master's word in the "spirit of altruism" (358). "Our ancestors," he assures an audience, "were free from pride, envy, crime and luxury" (514), and "there was no jealousy and hatred in the Aryan consciousness" (295). But the colonizers soon corrupted these beautiful Buddhist children of Lanka so that they fell into indolence, superstition, and servility.

In fact, Dharmapala's ancestors were very likely no more free of envy and pride than anyone else's, and, as we have seen in chapter 3, historians describe early Sri Lankan society as complex and plural rather than homogeneous. Still, however fanciful, Dharmapala's idealized version of the past is not harmful in itself; the problem arises when his golden-age utopianism combines with a universalizing religious vision to champion a specific, modern, Sri Lankan national and cultural identity.

As I have pointed out in chapters 1 and 2, the Buddha realized that his main practical task when engaging with others was to negotiate effectively between the ideal and actual, between his own core teachings and ordinary people's behavior that is always shot through with prejudice, resentment, fear, pride, and the like— the very things that Dharmapala says his forebears did not have. In the Discourses, the Buddha effects such a negotiation through dialogue not only with a wide range of individuals, but also with the Vedic traditions that were the nurturing ground of his own message. He does so through a combination of tact and insight constituting what I have called the literary dimension of the Discourses as distinct from the enunciation of doctrine in conceptual language. By contrast, though Dharmapala realizes that there is an urgent need to bring the Buddha's teachings to a demoralized people, he does not follow the Buddha's example by attempting to show his audiences how to discover their own particular resistance to the spirit of the *Dhamma* by bringing their prejudices to the surface and enabling a conscious transcendence of deep-set, traditional divisions of caste, kin-group, or ethnicity. Instead, Dharmapala looked to science to effect the necessary mediation. As we see, he praises Buddhism especially for being "scientific," and he looks to modern science and technology to provide the means for putting the downtrodden Sinhalas back in touch with a pure, progressive Buddhism, free of superstition. For Dharmapala, science rather than dialogical complexity mediates between the ideal and the actual, and, as we see, in the name of science he annexes to Buddhism a theory of race based on what he thought evolutionary biology to be.

Dharmapala's inability to reproduce or imitate the dialogical complexities of the Pali Canon, together with his commitment to modern science can help to explain the remarkable, sometimes obstinate, literal-mindedness that pervades his written work. For instance, after broadly dismissing Jesus's teachings because they contain "nothing especially sublime," Dharmapala goes on to say that the parables show Jesus to be "a man of limited knowledge." As evidence, Dharmapala claims that "no sower in Asia would go sowing seeds on barren and rocky ground," and it is bad advice "to allow the tares and the wheat to grow together" (448). Elsewhere he concludes that, for similar reasons, the "parables about the mustard seed, the sower, the wheat and tares are absurd" (499–500). As with his reading of the Pali Canon, he does not consider the function of metaphor or the affective power and complexity of the writing. The parables, after all, are frequently disconcerting, counterintuitive, and full of intimations of an eschatological event (the Kingdom) that will overturn our usual expectations and cause us to realize how urgently we are called to faith. But Dharmapala does not notice any of that, and to read the parables as literally as he does is, simply, to be a poor reader.

Dharmapala's characteristic literal-mindedness would be less significant were it not that he applies it to the *Mahavamsa*'s mythic stories of origin, and to modern science, which he thought the best means of bringing a true Buddhism to the demoralized Sinhalas. As we have now, these days, increasingly good reason to realize, science does not seem likely any time soon to solve a wide range of human problems, and our anxieties about death and suffering, our insecurity, fraught relationships, hopes, and desires do not as yet yield to scientifically objective solutions. As we have seen, the Buddha's Discourses can insightfully remind us that oversimplifying the moral lives of human beings does not help them on the way to liberation, but rather the reverse, and yet, in his optimism about science we might feel that Dharmapala indulges just such an oversimplification.

Still, despite the fact that his writing is rarely (if ever) subtle, Dharmapala is often passionate and forceful. Thus, for instance, he is unabashedly contemptuous of a world where, as he says, "the majority of the people are half insane and easily imposed upon by charlatans," and where, consequently, "religions are advertised like 'Pears Soap,' 'Dwar's Whisky,' 'Beechan's Pills,' 'Zambuk,' 'Sanatogan' and 'Eno's Furit [sic] Salt'" (217). There is some verve in this feisty, if heavy-handed, show of verbal aggression, which is wholly characteristic of Dharmapala's frequent satirical diatribes, especially against the colonizers. As always, he can be counted on to brandish his walking stick at an audience.

So far, I have been arguing that Dharmapala's substitution of scientific objectivity and directness for dialogical complexity and indirection leads him uncritically to declare the racial purity of the Sinhalas as basic to the restoration of a lost golden age of Sinhala Buddhism. One result of Dharmapala's commitment to this all-too clear agenda is that he prepares the way for indignation and anger to be directed against any non-Sinhala group unwilling to accept a Sinhala Buddhist Sri Lanka. After independence, the Tamils were first in line among such groups, and the national hero, Dutthagamini, had already provided an example of how to deal with an earlier version of the same threat. By a terrible irony, the warfare, anger, prejudice, and pride of caste that Dharmapala denounces in universal terms now return by way of the "*Mahavamsa* mentality" to energize a cultural Buddhism imagined in quasi-scientific terms and reproducing the very exclusivism from which the Buddha wanted to deliver all of humankind. This process is, again, what I mean by regressive inversion, which occurs when a passionate commitment to the transcendent is reinvested in a group identity from which the commitment to transcendence itself should liberate us. The means by which regressive inversion takes hold even of our best intentions are as elusive as they are dangerous and, in Dharmapala's case, despite his highly remarkable achievements, the very least we might wish is that he had been a better reader, especially of the Discourses of his own beloved Pali Canon.

To conclude, I would like to cite a letter written by Dharmapala after his arrest and internment in India in connection with the 1915 Buddhist-Muslim riots in Sri Lanka. Dharmapala points out that he was absent from the island in 1913 and 1914. Moreover, his writings during that period "would testify I had only one idea and that is to reform the Sinhalese people." He goes on:

> I have severely criticized the Buddhist priesthood, and the laymen,
> and I believe I became the object of their hatred on account of the
> criticisms that I leveled against them. Among the Sinhalese I do not
> think I could count two friends, because of my sledge hammer attacks.
> It is a mistake to think that my writings had anything to do with the
> riots. (722)

Although the British interned Dharmapala unjustly, they knew they had cause
for concern, and that Dharmapala's Buddhist revival was shaping into a powerful political force. Dharmapala himself was a firebrand and a subversive, and
the British wanted him kept away from the volatile situation in Sri Lanka.
Yet there is something naïve (not, I think, faux-naïve) in Dharmapala's defense, not least because his letter carries a message that is the opposite of what
he intends.

Dharmapala correctly describes his attacks on the Sinhalas as "sledge hammer"; as we have seen, he criticizes *bhikkhus* and laypeople unsparingly, declaring them inferior to virtually every group to whom he compares them. This is
his way of demonstrating how far the Sinhalas have fallen from the ideal Buddhist kingdom in which their ancestors lived "free from pride, envy, crime and
luxury" (514). He keeps saying that he wants to awaken the Sinhalas from their
torpor, and he repeatedly satirizes their present moral corruption, drunkenness,
Western dress, shallow education, and superstitious practices. In short, he
makes them feel as badly about themselves as he can, but we should not think
that he does so for any other reason than to convert that damaged self-esteem
into indignation and protest against those who caused it to happen. In all this,
Dharmapala is a good deal more like an Old Testament prophet than he would
care to admit, given his distaste for the Hebrew Scriptures. He says uncomfortable things to his people and expects that they might react against him with
"hatred" until they understand that he is not the enemy, but a prophetic voice
showing them who the enemy really is. Poor self-esteem can rapidly engender
vindictiveness, and Dharmapala's castigation of the Sinhalas is not intended to
keep them subservient to the British, but to turn them into indignant activists.
Just so, Dharmapala's promotion of the Buddhist revival aims also at bringing
about a new sense of ethnic and national solidarity, bent on purifying the tribe
and getting rid of the hated colonizers.

Dharmapala's letter invites such a reading, but, literal-minded as ever,
Dharmapala himself seems unaware of it, or of the extent to which he was confirming rather than allaying the concerns of the British authorities by assuring
them that he has been the Sinhalas' harshest critic. Here and elsewhere, he does
not realize how caught up he is in the processes whereby a universal aspiration,
valued because it liberates us from narrow and dangerous prejudices, can be

deployed in ways that inflame those same prejudices, making them even more dangerous. The Pali Canon is well aware of the problem, as is evident in the Buddha's deployment of complex rhetorical strategies to bring unconscious prejudices into the light of day, so that we might understand how they impede liberation. By contrast, Dharmapala remained unaware of the dangers implicit in his particular brand of modernist Buddhism, and of the bitter harvest that it would produce. In substituting science for critical discernment, Dharmapala overlooked the fact that imagination is a moral force without which we do not sufficiently understand or acknowledge the dangers often implicit in our own best intentions.

CHAPTER 5

WALPOLA RAHULA
AND GAMINI SALGADO

BUDDHISM, DIALOGUE,
AND THE POLITICAL IMAGINARY

Walpola Rahula was highly influential in the modern Buddhist revival mainly because of his efforts to politicize the *bhikkhus*, whom he encouraged to protest directly against the colonial power. Rahula's aim was to return the *Sangha* to its rightful, preeminent place as the custodian of a national religion concerned for the people's welfare. Although his reforms were broadly in the tradition of Dharmapala, Rahula (as we shall see) developed a distinct agenda reflecting his own circumstances and personality. Nonetheless, both men agreed about the basic problem: colonialism had seriously demoralized the Sinhalas and had reduced Buddhism to an ineffectual set of ritual observances.

Rahula was an accomplished scholar with impressive international connections and a sophisticated understanding of ideas and religious traditions other than his own. In a widely read book, *What the Buddha Taught*, he wrote magisterially yet accessibly, praising the Buddha's tolerance, compassion, and universalism while unequivocally denouncing violence and war. By contrast, in a later book, *The Heritage of the Bhikkhu*, Rahula produced a virtual manifesto for a Sinhala Buddhist nationalism, linking the identity of the Sinhalas with the land and religion, and declaring a willingness to resort to violence to defend the Sinhala interest.

In the following pages, I am concerned with how Rahula reconciles his scholarly understanding of the Buddha's core teachings with the claims of a passionately felt, Dharmapala-inspired, Sinhala nationalism. To this end, he resorted especially to an intellectual strategy claiming that different historical circumstances call for changes in how the Buddha's message should be interpreted. He argued that relativism of this type is exemplified by the Pali Canon, and, most notably, he appealed to the needs of the historical moment to justify the rereading of Buddhism in the *Mahavamsa*, and in the construction of his own activist agenda.

As part of his promotion of the Sinhala Buddhist cause, Rahula (again like Dharmapala) attacked traditional Buddhist practices, which he saw as superstitious. Yet his lack of sympathy for popular tradition suggests something of his own inability to imagine the needs of ordinary people and how the Buddha's teachings might be communicated to the richly diverse society that Rahula wished to reform. To show something of the day-to-day Buddhist observances of the kind that drew only Rahula's impatience, I want to look briefly at Gamini Salgado's memoir, *The True Paradise*.

The Buddhism that was loosely woven into Salgado's family life as he grew up in Sri Lanka in the years preceding independence was less a matter of prescription than of well-tried communal practice—flexible, often humorous, and sometimes inconsistent. I consider Salgado's memoir in order to suggest that if Rahula is to write effectively about how Buddhism engages with the lives of actual people, he needs something of what Salgado shows us about the complexities of those lives. Yet Salgado's richly textured evocation of a traditional Buddhism also needs something of Rahula's political and social conscience if Salgado is to do more than provide a colorful memoir about growing up Buddhist. Once again, we are reminded that a dialogical interplay between precept and practice, prescriptive truth-claims and compassionate engagement would best embody the spirit of an authentic Buddhism. Let me now begin by saying a little about the relationship between the Buddhist revival and what is sometimes described as "traditional" Buddhist practice.

In an important analysis, Richard Gombrich[1] makes a distinction between two main types of Sri Lankan Buddhism, which he labels "modern" and "traditional." He is especially interested in the traditional, which, he argues, has scarcely changed in 1,500 years—that is, since the period of the fifth-century commentaries in which Sri Lankan Theravada Buddhism was consolidated. Although the polar opposition between Gombrich's two types is less clear-cut in experience than in theory, the distinction nonetheless effectively describes a broad, historically significant development within Buddhism in twentieth-century Sri Lanka.

To clarify the distinction, Gombrich points out that Sri Lankan Buddhists by and large subscribe to the basic teachings of the Pali Canon about *anatta* and *nibbana*, but in practice most do not aspire to *nibbana* in their lifetimes, but to a good rebirth.[2] In short, ordinary people tend to go on thinking of themselves as persons who will survive their death, and the austere, disjunctive canonical teachings about *anatta* and *nibbana* are frequently interpreted in ways that allow an accommodating engagement with the complexities, hopes, fears, and circumstances of everyday life and culture.

In this context, Gombrich describes a range of "traditional" lay practices aimed at acquiring merit for a good rebirth. These include making pilgrimages, participating in festivals and other rituals, giving donations to support the *Sangha*, believing in and propitiating various minor and local deities (many of them Hindu), and so on. The intricacies of abstract doctrine and the rigors of meditation are left largely to the *bhikkhus* who also provide ritual services for the laity, from whom otherwise they remain apart. Traditional Buddhism, then, is culturally conservative and ritually based, and accommodates a wide range of local beliefs and practices. By contrast, Gombrich describes modernist Buddhism as impatient of ritual divorced from socially responsible action; it emphasizes the role of the laity, blurring the distinction between the people and the *Sangha*; it is practical and embraces the idea that education is the key to technological and industrial progress. As we have seen in chapter 4, Dharmapala spearheaded this modernist movement, and Gombrich rightly points out how radically it departs from older practices and assumptions.

With this set of contrasts in mind, I now want to look mainly at Rahula's *The Heritage of the Bhikkhu*,[3] which, as I have mentioned, is a highly influential text in the modernist tradition, written as part of a program to encourage Sinhalese Buddhist monks to engage directly in politics and liberate Sri Lanka from British rule. *The Heritage of the Bhikkhu* was published in 1946 (English translation, 1974), and, as Seneviratne says, it is "a work that has influenced the monkhood more than any other in the recent history of Sri Lankan Theravada Buddhism. Indirectly, it also influenced in critical ways the society as a whole."[4]

In contrast to Rahula, and as an example of the texture of Buddhist life and experience that Gombrich describes as traditional, I want to consider Gamini Salgado's *The True Paradise*,[5] which was published posthumously (Salgado died in 1985), and recounts the author's early and teenage years in Sri Lanka until his departure in 1947. Eventually, Salgado became professor of English at the University of Exeter, and an expert in D. H. Lawrence and in English Renaissance drama. His memoir was well received by Sri Lankan and English reviewers, and offers a vivid account of traditional Buddhism in the years just prior to independence—that is, the same period in which Rahula's modernist manifesto, *The Heritage of the Bhikkhu*, was also produced.

WALPOLA RAHULA AND BHIKKHU ACTIVISM

Walpola Rahula (1907–1997)[6] was born in the Galle district of the Southern Province of Sri Lanka. As a teenager, he entered the *Sangha*, where he received a traditional monastic education, and, in 1936, he was the first *bhikkhu* to enroll in the Ceylon University College, a newsworthy event that, we are assured, was "not appreciated by some conservative elements."

Rahula began to study English when he was about twenty years old, and was assisted by Dr. E. F. C. Ludowyck, a lecturer and, later, professor of English. His studies of mathematics were assisted by another lecturer, Mr. S. Thangarajah, and, as Mallawarachchi points out, these two friends "are non-Sinhalese and non-Buddhist, indicating that he [Rahula] was regarded and appreciated as a person whose interests were not confined to any religious or national boundaries."[7] Throughout his life, Rahula would frequently be admired by acquaintances as ecumenically broad-minded; thus, we are assured in a typical encomium that he was "possessed by qualities of mind and character which have transcended what specifically belongs to any group or religion."[8]

As an undergraduate, Rahula was involved in student affairs and enjoyed reading Chaucer and Shakespeare. He also allowed himself to watch dress rehearsals of the University Dramatic Society; although he realized it would be inappropriate for a *bhikkhu* to attend an actual performance, he found a way to interpret the rules to allow him to watch plays anyway. As a matter of principle, Rahula would continue to hold that traditional religious practices need to adapt to changing times and circumstances, and, as we shall see, this would become a key argument in his interpretation of modernist Buddhism.

In the 1930s, Rahula had already declared himself a critic of traditional Buddhist observances and practices and, through preaching and pamphleteering, he recommended a renewed concern among *bhikkhus* for the public good, broadly along the lines set out by Dharmapala. A decade later, Rahula would support workers' strikes and renew his call for the *bhikkhus* to become politically engaged, and in this context he wrote *Bhiksuvage Urumaya* (1946), later translated as *The Heritage of the Bhikkhu* (1974). Although this polemical book reflects the interests of a group of like-minded activists, it overlaps in significant ways with Rahula's doctoral thesis on the early history of Buddhism in Sri Lanka, later published as *History of Buddhism in Ceylon* (1956).

In 1943, Rahula visited India to further his studies at the University of Calcutta and, in 1945, he returned to Sri Lanka to read for his doctorate at the University of Ceylon. He was also appointed to teach at the Vidyalankara Pirivena, a seedbed for the so-called political *bhikkhus*, and the context within which he hurriedly composed *The Heritage of the Bhikkhu*. This combative, pungently argued book maintains that before the arrival of the European colonizers, the *Sangha* had been socially engaged and actively concerned about the welfare of the people. The British especially deprived the *Sangha* of its social role, and as a result the *bhikkhus* became reclusive. Only with independence from colonial rule would the *Sangha* be restored to its proper social function.

In 1950, Rahula went to Paris to study Mahayana Buddhism at the Sorbonne. He worked on the fourth-century Buddhist philosopher, Asanga, mainly with Professor Paul Demiéville, and became closely acquainted also with a distinguished group of European scholars. In 1958, as a delegate to the UNESCO General Conference, he met Angelo Roncalli, later Pope John XXIII. At a reception at the Vatican Embassy in Paris, Roncalli, then Papal Nuncio, greeted Rahula, proclaiming: "This is the real ambassador! No frontier for him; no nationalities. This is Buddhist wisdom!"[9] Not long afterward, Rahula published *What the Buddha Taught* (1959), a much-praised, highly expert and accessible introduction to Buddhism, now translated into several languages. As even a cursory reading makes clear, *What the Buddha Taught* confirms Roncalli's praise for Rahula as an ambassador for a true Buddhist wisdom, beyond frontiers.

In 1964, Professor Edmund F. Perry of Northwestern University was instrumental in bringing Rahula to the United States where he accepted a post at Northwestern as Bishop Brashares Professor of History and Literature of Religions. Perry, a Methodist minister, developed a close friendship with Rahula, again confirming Rahula's ability to communicate effectively across religious and cultural boundaries.

In 1966, Rahula returned to Sri Lanka as vice-chancellor of Vidyodaya University. Three years later, he resigned and returned to Paris. In 1974, he moved to London, where he continued his studies, virtually in retirement. He died in 1997.

As this outline suggests, there are two broad aspects to Rahula's life and work. The first is sophisticated, international, ecumenical, and scholarly; the second is polemical, specifically Sri Lankan, and focused on Sinhala nationalism. Three main considerations can help to explain Rahula's attempts to reconcile these two contrasting sides of his life and work. First is his scholarly conviction that the Buddha intended his teachings to be adapted to fit changing historical circumstances. Second is his interpretation of Buddhism by way of the *Mahavamsa*, as the revered chronicle is deployed once again to support a reading of modern Sri Lankan history in which the special destiny of the Sinhalas is emphasized. Third is Rahula's poor opinion of traditional Buddhist practices and his consequent, overly optimistic reliance on theory at the expense of an adequate imagination of the actual complexity of people and events. Let us first consider Rahula's ecumenism and internationalism, which are especially clear in his popular book, *What the Buddha Taught*.

In general, *What the Buddha Taught*[10] is clear and accessible, and Rahula's explanations of the main Buddhist doctrines are temperate and carefully considered. He assures us that "the freedom of thought allowed by the Buddha is unheard of elsewhere in the history of religions," and he declares such freedom "necessary" because, although the Buddha shows us the way to liberation, "we must tread the Path ourselves" (2) and must be convinced individually of the value of doing so. To this end, we should "examine even the Tathagata (Buddha) himself" (3), and this same freedom of enquiry should be extended to other religions. Rahula reminds us that the Buddha's teaching is based on a "vast conception of universal love and compassion for all living beings" and each of us is to develop "compassion (*karuna*) . . . and wisdom (*panna*)" (46) in equal measure. Consequently, "violence in any form, under any pretext whatsoever, is absolutely against the teaching of the Buddha" (5). Later, Rahula reconfirms the point: "Buddhism advocates and preaches non-violence and peace as its universal message, and does not approve of any kind of violence or destruction of life." Accordingly, "there is nothing that can be called a 'just war'— which is only a false term coined and put into circulation to justify and excuse hatred, cruelty, violence and massacre" (84).

Rahula comments also on the Buddha's method of teaching through dialogue. He tells us that because the Buddha was highly practical, he did not answer questions without considering how "to help the questioner on the way to realization." Consequently, the Buddha bore in mind people's "standard of development, their tendencies, their mental make-up, their character, their capacity to understand" (63). As an example, Rahula cites the Buddha's silence in response to a question asked by Vacchagotta on the nature of the self. Rahula concludes that "silence seems to have had much more effect" than "any eloquent answer or discussion" (64), because the Buddha realized that Vacchagotta would not be capable of following a detailed argument and would become confused. But although Rahula notices the Buddha's dialogical engagement with others, he does not dwell on the topic, nor does he imitate the Buddha's method in his own writing. Admittedly, it is unfair to expect Rahula to do such a thing, given that *What the Buddha Taught* is intended to offer a clear description of the Buddha's core ideas, but it is worth noticing that Rahula appreciates this aspect of the Buddha's teaching method.

The contrast between *What the Buddha Taught* and *The Heritage of the Bhikkhu* registers immediately, even on a casual reading. Yet Rahula did not move directly from the first of these books to the second; rather the composition of *The Heritage of the Bhikkhu* overlapped with Rahula's immensely learned *History of Buddhism in Ceylon*,[11] which covers the period from the third century B.C.E. until the tenth century C.E. Basically, the *History of Buddhism in Ceylon* draws on the *Mahavamsa* to describe a relationship of mutual support between the *Sangha* and the monarchy within the "Buddhist nation" (264). Rahula stresses the contribution of the *bhikkhus* in ancient times to the welfare and education of the Sri Lankan people, and argues that the establishment of Buddhism was vital to the prosperity of "a whole civilization" (59). Buddhism "became the state religion from the day of its introduction into the Island," and retained this privileged position until "the end of the Sinhalese rule in the 19th century A.C." (62). The decisive change came with the ascendancy of the British, and in *The Heritage of the Bhikkhu*, Rahula expands especially upon this point, as he accuses the British of breaking the relationship between the *Sangha* and the state, thereby undermining the social role of the *bhikkhus* and ensuring the decline of Buddhism.

This set of arguments deriving from the *Mahavamsa* and marshalled against colonialism is familiar from Dharmapala, and, throughout the Buddhist revival, the *Mahavamsa* continued to offer a means of appropriating Buddhism to the cause of modern Sinhala nationalism. For his part, Rahula made the transition from *What the Buddha Taught* to *The Heritage of the Bhikkhu* by way of his *History*, in which, as we see, he sets out his own version of a *Mahavamsa*-inspired attack on colonialism. Clearly, Dharmapala is an important precursor, but Rahula does not mention him often, and there are important differences between them. For instance, Dharmapala's *bhikkhu* remains, as Seneviratne says, "an ascetic and humble soldier," whereas Rahula's *bhikkhu* "is a powerful kingmaker who is heavily endowed or salaried and lives in comfort."[12] This difference reflects Rahula's ideological program for a politically powerful *Sangha*, as distinct from Dharmapala's more modest concern for the simple life and adequate living standards. In both the *History of Buddhism in Ceylon* and *The Heritage of the Bhikkhu*, Rahula defends the *Sangha*'s accumulation of wealth and endowments, and he does so by resorting to his favorite argument that rules governing the monastic life need to change with the times: "Adapt or perish,"[13] as he succinctly puts it. That is, for Rahula, history itself requires that the Buddha's teachings be reinterpreted so that Buddhism will not "perish," and Rahula is prepared to take whatever steps are required to ensure that Buddhism remains historically significant and politically engaged, as the *Mahavamsa* prescribes.

Still, in the *History of Buddhism in Ceylon* we are frequently reminded also of the discriminating author of *What the Buddha Taught*, and the *History* is less directly polemical than *The Heritage of the Bhikkhu*. For instance, Rahula acknowledges that the *Mahavamsa* "is embellished with poetic diction and imagery" (xxiii) and should be interpreted circumspectly. With this in mind, he cautions readers that an anecdote about a particular *bhikkhu* "cannot be taken as literally true" (260), and he provides an interpretation of various "poetically expressed statements" (38) about *yakkhas*. Again, he reminds us that Buddhism is "purely a personal religion," and its "establishment" as the state religion is "quite foreign to the teaching of the Buddha" (54). Also, he warns against idealizing the past because "in reality" the ideal "never existed" and "drifts further and further away like a mirage as one draws near it" (199).

As with his acknowledgment of the Buddha's dialogical method of teaching, we might notice here that Rahula does not really see the implications of these discriminating observations for his own main argument. For instance, his warnings about not taking the *Mahavamsa* too literally do not prevent him from accepting the historical accuracy of the accounts about Vijaya and Mahinda, and his understanding of basic Buddhist teachings to the contrary does not prevent him from arguing for Buddhism as a state religion. Nor does his awareness that we tend to idealize the past prevent him from doing just that in an account of the "happy and healthy" lives of the *bhikkhus* "in early days" (204). Not surprisingly, contradictions such as these between precept and practice stand out especially when Rahula turns to the Dutthagamini epic.

Dutthagamini, we learn, is "the greatest national hero of early Buddhist Ceylon," and Rahula provides an enraptured account of why this is so:

> The entire Sinhalese race was united under the banner of the young Gamani. This was the beginning of nationalism among the Sinhalese. It was a new race with healthy young blood, organized under the new order of Buddhism. A kind of religio-nationalism, which almost amounted to fanaticism, roused the whole Sinhalese people. (79).

Under the influence of Rahula's modernist agenda, Buddhism and the "Sinhalese race" are conflated here in a "religio-nationalism" as unsettling as it is intense. Rahula goes on to mention Dutthagamini's moment of misgiving about the number of enemy dead, and cites the reassurance provided by the eight arahants that only one and a half human beings had been killed. Rahula makes no comment on the episode other than to say, deadpan: "Thus orthodox religious opinion encouraged Buddhist nationalism" (80). It is as if he closes his eyes to the conviction to which he gives such unequivocally strong expression in *What the Buddha Taught*, that Buddhism and violence are incompatible, and there can be no just war. His own silence suggests a moral imagination in abeyance, a sort of parody of the Buddha's silence which Rahula construed as a way to avoid confusing Vacchagotta. Here, one might wonder why Rahula does not notice the difference between his understanding of what the Buddha taught and his loyalty to the national cause of the Sinhalas. Similar disturbing effects occur throughout *The Heritage of the Bhikkhu*,[14] in which Rahula combines his *Mahavamsa*-based account of Sinhala Buddhist history with an urgent call for the *bhikkhus* to become active in modern politics.

Rahula begins *The Heritage of the Bhikkhu* by asserting that "Buddhism is based on service to others" (3), and this claim remains central to his desire that the *Sangha* should be socially engaged. But Rahula realizes that he cannot simply return to the past; conditions now are different, and again he insists that Buddhism needs to adjust accordingly. And so, once more he marshals his favored argument, pointing out that already in the Pali Canon the Buddha makes allowances for rules to be changed "to suit occasions and circumstances" (9). Rahula then provides a series of examples from which he concludes that "the *Vinaya* (the Code of Disciplinary Rules for the *Sangha*) is not an absolute truth; it is only a convention agreed upon for the orderly and smooth life of a social organization" (11). Because changes in "social organization" require equivalent changes in the *Sangha*'s rules of discipline, Rahula is able to explain how the *bhikkhus* could amass great wealth, and how they came to serve as teachers, political advisors, artists, medical practitioners, and the like. But with colonialism—beginning with the Portuguese (1505), who were followed by the Dutch (1658) and the British (1796)—Buddhism lost is social relevance and "its original purity" (59). The British were especially effective in introducing laws that encouraged the separation of *bhikkhus* from the laity; as a result, the *Sangha* lost touch with modern social developments, and the *bhikkhus* became "useless to society" because "laymen had nothing to learn from them" (91). Subsequently, the *bhikkhus* retreated to "an idle, cloistered life in the temple" (91), and their activities were limited to chanting *pirit*, conducting funeral rites, and other ceremonies. For Rahula, this was a "calamity," though even in the worst of times the *bhikkhus* never quite forgot that their "noblest heritage" was the "glory of the Buddhist culture and civilization of the Sinhala nation" (92). But now the time has come for "a few Buddhist monks of heroic character intent on reviving the nation and its religion" (93) to set in motion reforms that will combine Sri Lanka's ancient heritage with "the modern world and international requirements" (97).

As this summary suggests, Rahula especially deplores colonialism, and the chapters in which he cites memoranda from British officials and documents recording the contempt in which Christian missionaries held "the Superstition of Boodhoo" (84), are searing, to say the least. Rahula wisely lets the evidence stand without much explication, but it is clearly central to his case that the liberation of Sri Lanka from colonial oppression is also the liberation of Sri Lankan Buddhism, if only because it is axiomatic that "the nation and the religion have to move together" (95).

To confirm this point, Rahula never tires of proclaiming that Buddhism defines the Sinhalese people; it is "the national religion" and "the heritage of the Sinhala people and of their land" (16). A thirteenth-century commentary is cited with approval, to the effect that the "island of Lanka belongs to the Buddha himself," and consequently "the residence of false believers in this island will never be permanent" (18). To the ancient inhabitants of Sri Lanka it was evident also that "a Sinhalese had to be a Buddhist," and Christian missionaries are blamed for treating national development as "something apart from religious development" (92).

Again, the *Mahavamsa* is a main source of inspiration for such a vision of the past. Rahula cites it often, and especially to praise Dutthagamini, "the greatest of national heroes." In his decisive battle against Elara, Dutthagamini was able "to liberate the nation and the religion from the foreign yoke" (20), and Rahula recounts how Dutthagamini carried a relic of the Buddha on his spear, and, inspired by his example and inflamed with "national ardour" (21), a group of monks put off their robes and joined his army. "From this time," Rahula concludes, "the patriotism and the religion of the Sinhalese became inseparably linked" (21), and the *bhikkhus* considered it a "sacred duty" (22) to serve their country, even by participating in warfare.

As we have seen, Rahula claims repeatedly that rules of behavior need to change with the times—the *Vinaya*, as we have seen "is not an absolute truth." At first, he deploys this idea to explain minor changes to regulations about food, drink, and clothing, but, as the argument develops, so too does the scope of the appeal to changing circumstances, as, for instance, when he offers to explain the acquisition of vast monastic wealth, property holdings (35), and even the keeping of slaves (37).

Yet at one point, Rahula hesitates. He had just summarized the *Mahavamsa* account of Dutthagamini's victory over Elara, and is considering Dutthagamini's remorse about the large number of enemy dead. He cites the advice offered by the *arahants*:

> By this deed there is no obstruction to thy way to Heaven. Only one and a half human beings have been slain here, O Lord of men. The one had taken the [three] refuges [taken the Buddha, *Dhamma*, and *Sangha* as refuges], the other had taken on himself the five precepts [*panca-sila*]. Unbelievers and men of evil life were the rest, not more to be esteemed than beasts. (21–22)

Commenting on this statement, Rahula declares flatly that it "is diametrically opposed to the teaching of the Buddha" (22), and wonders if the *bhikkhus* really did say such a thing. But he then promptly drops the point, noticing instead that the controversial advice given to Dutthagamini really shows how thoroughly Mahanama, the compiler, had accepted the idea that "for the freedom and uplift of the religion and the country," even "the destruction of human beings . . . was not a very grave crime" (22). Rahula does not return to the problem of contradicting the Buddha's teachings; instead, he confirms the conclusion imputed to Mahanama and other "ordinary *bhikkhus* and laymen" (22), that it is a "sacred duty" to serve the country and its religion, even by going to war. His initial uneasiness seems again to be assuaged by the idea that the rules of behaviour have changed, but he has moved far from the minor adjustments regarding clothes and food that he finds in the Pali Canon. Those examples are the thin end of a wedge that has now been driven far enough to compromise some of the most distinctive Buddhist teachings about nonviolence, nonpossessiveness, and how irrelevant are distinctions of caste, kin, tribe, or nation to the realization of *nibbana*.

Rahula's remarks about Dutthagamini's remorse are especially interesting because they show how Rahula can acknowledge a problem without imagining its implications, so that he ends up expressing an exclusionism of which he often seems unaware, as we see frequently in the *Heritage of the Bhikkhu*. For instance, we learn that some Tamil kings ruled in Sri Lanka as Buddhists, but "probably they preferred to be Buddhists for political convenience" (19). When Sri Lanka was in decline during the Portuguese period, the seaports were "dominated by the Moslems" (55), a fact that is itself prima facie evidence of the decline in question. Under the Dutch, "Many Buddhists embraced Protestantism for no other reason than that of obtaining employment" (61). Later, under the British, "for the sake of materialistic gains, many Sinhalese embraced Christianity" (90). Surely it would be worth mentioning that a Tamil could be a genuine Buddhist, that a Moslem trader could be an asset, and that some Sinhalese could become Christian for religious reasons rather than for material gain. Instead, Rahula's imagined Sinhala Buddhist nationalism is such a driving force throughout his argument that he gives no thought to how intolerant he often sounds, and we lose sight, here, of the sophisticated intellectual, admired as an ambassador for a Buddhism without frontiers.

In the foregoing account I have suggested that it is possible to see Rahula in two main, contrasting ways. On the one hand, he is an ecumenical, tolerant internationalist who writes elegantly about the Buddha's universal message; on the other hand, he is an ideologue for whom Buddhism is identified with the "Sinhalese race" and with a nationalist political agenda. Rahula found his way from the first of these positions to the second by means of his historical study of ancient Ceylon, which includes a *Mahavamsa*-inspired account of Sinhala Buddhism, marshalled to challenge colonial rule. He reconciles his nationalist interpretation of the *Mahavamsa* with the Buddhism that he describes in *What the Buddha Taught* by appealing to a principle of relativity, claiming that the Buddha's teachings, as well as regulations governing the *Sangha*, need to change with the times. The way then lies open for Rahula to call for a militant, nationalist Buddhism in which the Buddha's universal vision is appropriated to serve the special interests of the Sinhalas.

So far, I have dealt with Rahula's historically based argument about the principle of relativity and how it combines with his interpretation of the *Mahavamsa*. The third consideration that I mentioned as significant in helping to explain the development of Rahula's *bhikkhu* activisim is his poor opinion of traditional Buddhist practices. The problem here is that Rahula does not much identify with the lives of ordinary people, and he is overly theoretical in his message about reform. As we have seen, the Buddha's Discourses show us how to negotiate precisely this kind of difficulty, while also offering a warning about how idealism can become oppressive if it is not mediated to others discerningly. To provide some idea of the kind of traditional Buddhist practice with which, I am claiming, Rahula is out of touch, let us now consider a quite different kind of book.

GAMINI SALGADO:
"HOMELY PRACTICE"

Gamini Salgado's *The True Paradise*[15] contains eight chapters, each a vignette describing a phase of the author's childhood and youth in Sri Lanka prior to his departure for England in 1947. Though the events described in this vivid and entertaining autobiographical memoir about growing up in a village near Colombo took place during the years when Rahula also was working on behalf of the causes described in *The Heritage of the Bhikkhu*, these two authors present us with quite different imagined worlds. This is the case not least because the traditional Buddhism evoked by Salgado is the very kind that Rahula deplores. Yet Salgado's memoir offers a compelling, heartwarming account of how sustaining, complex, and salutary a nonmodernist Buddhism might be.

Although his main topic is himself, Salgado's narrative voice is often refracted and ironic. For instance, his account of various marketplace hawkers (snake charmers, palm readers, ballad-sellers, and the like) is written with considerable verve, reproducing a child's enthusiasm, but also with a bemused appreciation for the child's impressionability as he encounters this colorful but highly dubious group of people. An example is the author's comment on the unkempt and raffish snakebite man, about whom Salgado says simply: "Without the cobra he would have been someone I'd laugh at or feel sorry for" (5). This is an adult reflection and does not occur to the child who actually encounters the snakebite man, not thinking about him apart from his fascinating stage prop. Throughout *The True Paradise* there are many such small, self-reflexive shifts in tone and perspective by means of which Salgado maintains a wry distance from experiences that nonetheless are sympathetically evoked. The result is a flexible judgment, hovering between participatory enthusiasm and ironic recollection.

A more provocative deployment of narrative voice and point of view occurs in Salgado's wonderfully detailed account of his parents' wedding. This was the marriage within which Salgado was later conceived, and so he did not witness it, but it is described as if he were there. For instance, we learn that his grandmother "embraced her daughter and sniffled wordlessly against her cheek" (71), and of his mother he says, there was "a tiny fleck of blood at the corner of her big toe" (70). The ceremony then is evoked in detail, and we are to deduce that the information was gathered later, in conversation with others after his mother's death, which is recounted in a later chapter.

The immediacy of the experience of his mother's death on the sixteen-year-old boy creates an effect interestingly in contrast to the vivid account of her wedding, even though the narrator was absent from the wedding and all too present at the time of her death. So, when his father tells him the bad news, the forlorn Gamini wanders through Colombo in a daze, with "only a kind of hollowness inside which made everything outside seem empty too" (121). He remembers events "vaguely" (123), as he wanders into a cinema and then returns later to see the same film again (126). "Curiously," he recalls, "I can remember almost nothing of the funeral itself, not even whether it was a burial or cremation" (138). This strange detail tells us a good deal about Salgado's authorial self-consciousness. If he was able to recover from others the exquisite details of his parents' wedding, surely it would be easy to discover whether his mother had been buried or cremated. Clearly, the main aim here is to render the disorientation caused by grief, by means of a certain inchoate quality in the narrative, just as the delight of the wedding is rendered by an intense focus on particulars. In short, Salgado's narrative strategies enable us to know and feel something of the intermittences and evolution of an interior life, and the flexibility of his authorial voice suggests a pliable and emergent, rather than a defined sense of self.

Not surprisingly, Salgado's world is permeated by the British colonial presence, but he does not thematize colonialism; rather, he lets us judge it from its myriad effects on his early life—for instance, encounters with government officials, the brand names of products, railway administration, the cinema, and (especially) the English books so coveted by his father and which afforded the young Salgado a special opportunity to learn the language in which he was eventually to make a distinguished academic career.

As he does with other topics, Salgado affords a range of viewpoints on colonialism. For instance, he is partly appreciative of what the British could offer, but he can also be caustic and satirical. Thus, the starchy official who attends his parents' wedding is dismissed as "an accident, necessary for the Government's purposes, a strange stranded fish" (73), and a new British manager of railways is hopelessly, comically overwhelmed by the teeming energy of the passengers he would regulate. Salgado's grandfather objects energetically to the need to learn English to get a government job ("the Government job he will get with his Ingiris and his bloody crucified Jesus" [61]); yet his father's proficiency in English does in fact enable secure employment, and so the account leaves us with both a protest and an accommodation.

In all this, the British influence is not depicted as merely oppressive, but as one element in an immensely varied and colorful world, filled with hawkers and beggars, *bhikkhus* and Tamils, Burghers and Sinhalese, peons, people of different castes and conditions, complex family relationships, colorful festivals and religious observances of various kinds. This many-sided world is the context within which Buddhism also is mainly represented.

Salgado's widow, Fenella Copplestone, describes his family's "Buddhist principles and homely practice of their faith," and says that these things shaped Gamini's "sense of the meaning of his existence" (175). Certainly, an acceptance of religion as part of the texture of day-to-day life emerges from many references to Buddhism throughout *The True Paradise*, coloring Salgado's world but without dominating it. Allusions to Buddhism thus mingle effortlessly with descriptions of street vendors, family celebrations, public holidays, child's play, marriage, and death, and, throughout, we come to know how religion can be a stabilizing, enriching influence, its contours fluid, its atmosphere genial, its precepts unimposing and often tempered by a carnivalesque unruliness.

For instance, the snakebite man curses his cobra in religious language (the Triple Gem, *kamma*, *samsara*, rebirth, and so on [6–9]). It is perfectly evident that this man is a scam artist and his conversation is frequently lewd; yet we are not to underestimate the appeal of his well-tried pitch, as he deploys the commonplaces of Buddhist piety in a manner that is irreverent but not entirely unserious or ineffective.

The vignette describing the snakebite man is placed next to one about a hawker of verse storybooks, who recites the stories on request. Most requests are for tales about the life and exploits of the Buddha, and Salgado confides that he "learned more Buddhist stories from the songbook seller than I did at Sunday school" (4). Still, Sunday school also is important, and there is a careful account of how he received instruction there in Sanskrit and Pali from a punctilious and severe *bhikkhu* ("I hated him with the boundless hatred of childhood"). Disconcertingly, after the lesson the boys head off "to tease the deaf-mute temple gardener" (43), and the point is made that strict religious instruction does not mean that the spirit of the religious message will be well enough understood.

Allusions to Buddhism can also be poignant, as in the ritually whispered condolence, "impermanence and sorrow" (124), offered by a stranger on learning about the boy's bereavement, and also in the children's voices singing about the Buddha at his parents' wedding (70). Elsewhere, Salgado reflects that the young Siddhattha Gotama's experiences of old age, disease, and death (from which his royal father attempted to protect him) are not "symbolic," as he once thought; rather, "remembering the teeming misshapen life on our road, I can see that the symbolism is only a heightened picture of the reality" (29). And a brief summary of how Buddhism is "the sum and staple of religion for us" (53) is elegant and effective, neither doctrinaire nor irreverent.

Not surprisingly, this tolerant, imprecisely defined traditional observance allows for inconsistencies, which for the most part are not taken too seriously, or too closely interrogated. Thus, when eggs are to be broken (54) the Salgado family sends them next door to a Christian household that does not share the Buddhist compunction about nonviolence to (potentially) unborn chickens. The broken eggs are then returned to the Salgados for use. Again, as a child, Salgado would not kill worms for fishing-bait but he uncovered them in the sand for his Christian pals to take and use (35). Even the monks are not beyond an artful dodge, putting the letter before the spirit. Because a monk should not ask for a second helping of food for himself, he asks on behalf of the monk seated next to him. The little ruse in turn is understood by the server at the communal feast, who then gives the petitioning monk what he (really) wants (47). Such things are allowed to be amusing, reassuringly part of a religious atmosphere that is flexible and nondoctrinaire.

Yet Salgado provides little information about Buddhist history or politics. At one point, describing a Vesak celebration, he notices the colorful tableaux depicting "not only scenes from Buddhist life, but also from Ceylon history," and explains that these are "inextricably entangled in the average Buddhist consciousness." "The founder of the Sinhalese race," he goes on to tell us, "according to a stubborn tradition, set foot on these shores the very day the Buddha passed away and the Buddha himself supposedly made three visits to Ceylon." But this topic is immediately dropped, and the account returns with gusto to "a marvellous tableau showing the prince Siddhartha leaping over the river on his white horse" (52). The "intricate entanglement" remains unexamined, and although the *Mahavamsa* is the source of the "stubborn tradition" in question, it is not mentioned, and the veracity of the "tradition" is left carefully undefined.

Throughout *The True Paradise*, Buddhism therefore is represented as part of the fabric of daily life, woven into it through the cries of street vendors, the appeals of beggars, the ministrations of astrologers, the activities of *bhikkhus*, the play of children, the celebration of marriage, and the grief of bereavement. But there is no reflection on Buddhist politics, or on the Sinhalese Buddhist nationalism that was gathering momentum during the years Salgado recalls. Although, after his mother's death, Salgado embraced Marxism briefly, his account is of a particular, confused personal experience combining protest and grief, and he does not discuss the position of Marxism in Sri Lankan society at large, or its relation to Buddhism (139). He does not have an opinion about such matters, and the complexly lived, traditional religious practices he describes are, we might feel, all the more vulnerable because of this omission—vulnerable, that is, to manipulation by those who would annex them or repudiate them for political purposes.

COMMON PRINCIPLES, CULTURAL DIFFERENCES

Rahula's *The Heritage of the Bhikkhu* and Salgado's *The True Paradise* imagine Buddhism in different ways, exemplifying the main contrast Gombrich describes between "traditional" and "modern." Also, these two books can represent two sides of a dialogue, each incomplete without the other.

As I have argued in chapters 1 and 2, although canonical Buddhism proposes a set of core beliefs, stated straightforwardly in the Four Noble Truths and clustering around the ideas of *anatta*, *kamma*, *samsara*, and *nibbana*, the complexity of our actual lives needs to be assessed in an intelligently imaginative way if we (or most of us) are to be brought to see the relevance to ourselves of the abstractly stated truth-claims. To lose the balance between these two poles—clear principles and lived complexities—is to invite problems that, if extrapolated into the political sphere, can rapidly become dangerous.

As we see, Rahula offers a telling critique of colonialism in the name of national liberation. His main argument is pragmatic, and his narrative voice is authoritative, committed, and representative of a political movement. Yet in the name of Sinhalese Buddhist nationalism, Rahula modifies his scholarly understanding of what the Buddha taught, taking it in the direction of a *Mahavamsa*-inspired version of Sri Lankan history. He does so by invoking a principle of historical relativity, by means of which he essentializes the Sinhalas. His position then becomes worryingly exclusionist, ignoring ethnic diversity and the complex day-to-day lives of actual Sri Lankan people. Certainly, for Rahula the omission of an adequately imagined complexity has unsettling consequences, evident mainly in an unawareness of the regressive inversion entailed by his annexing the Buddha's transcendent vision to a passionately felt national group interest. The horrors of violent ethnic conflict might have taught Rahula to think differently; so too might the Buddha's Discourses, which Rahula understood as well as anybody ever has, but which he was unable to imitate sufficiently well in his own writing.

By contrast, Salgado's memoir offers a vivid account of an actual Sinhalese family, full of vitality, contretemps, loveable absurdities, celebration, and grief. His narrative voice is flexible, refracted, ironic, and aware of life's inconsistencies and resistances to uniformity. Religion for him is less a matter of prescription than of tried communal practice, woven loosely but pervasively into people's lives and treated with a combination of respect and satire, seriousness and lightheartedness. Yet Salgado offers no considered critique of colonialism or of the truth-claims of Buddhism, and his book remains uncommitted to positions that could be stated conceptually and acted upon politically.

Somehow, an accommodation needs to be made between the positive elements in both of these texts if Buddhism is to be reimagined effectively in the political and cultural circumstances both books describe. This would mean that committed principles should be expressed, colonialism challenged, and the glories of a past cultural phase appropriately admired. But it would also mean that the irreducible particularity of people and their relationships—their lack of "purity" and consistency—should be acknowledged and managed in the manner exemplified by the Buddha himself, as we see in the Discourses. In short, Rahula and Salgado need one another, and in the cultural and political spheres in modern Sri Lanka (as also in various analogous polities from Northern Ireland to Lebanon) a rapprochement between the positions they exemplify remains basic to an effective integration of religion into political and cultural discourse, and also to an adequate understanding of the Buddha's own warnings against certain dangerous misapplications of his teaching.

CHAPTER 6

J. R. JAYEWARDENE

PLAYING WITH FIRE

During his long and eventful political career, Junius Richard Jayewardene, who became generally known as J. R.,[1] struggled to contain the civic violence that had gathered momentum in the years preceding his election as prime minister in 1977 and which continued during his career (as it still does). Tragically, J. R.'s policies ended up contributing to the disorder he wished to quell, and in the following pages I want to explain something of how his interpretation of Buddhism helped to impede the realization of the good society to which he aspired.

As with Walpola Rahula, J. R. embraced the principles of the Buddhist revival set out by Dharmapala, and he especially resented the suppression of Buddhist culture under colonialism. But unlike Dharmapala and Rahula, J. R. strongly resisted the politicization of the *Sangha* and was vehemently opposed to the type of activist *bhikkhu* favored by Rahula. Still, J. R. was not a thoroughgoing secularist; he aspired to a righteous society (*dharmistha*), embodying Buddhist values. Also, he promoted a Sinhala Buddhist cultural nationalism—for instance, by massive expenditures of state funds to support Buddhist cultural activities, including the restoration of monuments, temples, and other artifacts, and a project to bring the *Mahavamsa* up to date.

To his enemies, J. R. seemed Machiavellian and insufferably authoritarian; to his supporters he was a gifted negotiator and an effective leader tested to the extreme in difficult times. It is hard to decide clearly about J. R. one way or the other, and even his biographers acknowledge how enigmatic he remains. On the one hand, his genuine political gifts were overwhelmed by the passionate intensities of a conflict that had reached the boiling point before he became prime minister, and it is easy to feel that J. R. labored nobly against impossible odds. On the other hand, J. R.'s efforts to realize a nonviolent, righteous society included the promotion of a cultural Buddhist nationalism, and it is easy to conclude that J. R. ends up doing what he did not want the *bhikkhus* to do in actively promoting Sinhala hegemony. To enable some better understanding of the complexities of J. R.'s situation and achievements, let us first consider his biography, and the kind of Buddhist convictions he espoused.

RIGHTEOUS SOCIETY AND REALPOLITIK

J. R. was born in Colombo. His father, E. W. Jayewardene, was a Supreme Court judge, and his mother, Agnes Helen, was the daughter of Tudugala Don Philip Wijewardene and his wife Helena. J. R. was raised as an Anglican, and had a Scottish governess. He was a distinguished student at school and at university, where he studied law. During his student years, as his politics became increasingly nationalist, he also became interested in Buddhism. As it happened, his mother's family, the Wijewardenes, were ardent Buddhists, and under the influence especially of his uncle, Walter Wijewardene, J. R. (together with his younger brother Corbett) received instruction at a temple. While still an undergraduate, J. R. gave up his allegiance to Anglicanism and became a Buddhist. In 1935, he married Elina Rupersinge in an arranged marriage that assured his financial security. He continued to practice law for the next seven years, but by mid-1942 he had effectively given up his practice and directed his energies instead to public life.

In the early years of his marriage, J. R.'s Buddhist convictions strengthened, and he read widely, using English translations of the Pali Canon. Not surprisingly, his first involvement in public life was influenced by the Buddhist revival movement—specifically, through the Buddhist Theosophical Society and the All-Ceylon Buddhist Congress. As a member of the Buddhist Theosophical Society, J. R. discovered the legacy of Anagarika Dharmapala, and by and by became an office-bearer of the Dharmapala Trust.[2] Certainly, the anticolonial, activist, empirically oriented aspects of Dharmapala's Buddhism appealed strongly to J. R., as did the revival of Sinhala Buddhist cultural traditions suppressed under British rule. But J. R. strongly resisted the politicization of the *bhikkus*; instead he opted for the liberal secularism of D. S. Senanayake, with whom he worked in the Ceylon National Congress. Senanayake was a founding member of the UNP, formed in 1946 especially with the hope of developing a moderate political consensus during the period when arrangements were anxiously being worked out with Britain to secure Sri Lanka's independence.

In supporting Senanayake, J. R. had unwittingly set himself on a collision course with the major political movement that I have described in chapter 3, led by S. W. R. D. Bandaranaike[3] and resulting in the formation of the SLFP. Like J. R., Bandaranaike was raised in a pro-British Anglican family. He was educated at Oxford, and when he found that his sympathies lay with the Sri Lankan nationalist cause, he too gave up Anglicanism and became a Buddhist.

Like J. R., he was also a member of the Buddhist Theosophical Society, where he was, again, strongly influenced by Dharmapala. Yet, despite these similar experiences, the two men clashed when it became clear to J. R. that Bandaranaike was concerned to develop a populist political movement based on a Sinhala ethnic identity marked especially by Buddhism and the Sinhala language.

As I have pointed out in chapter 3, the politicization of the *bhikkhus* was encouraged by the SLFP, and reached a high point in 1956 when the SLFP swept to victory in a general election and Bandaranaike became prime minister. Politically radical *bhikkhus* who campaigned for Bandaranaike took as their charter the Vidyalankara Declaration.[4] This important, brief document, issued from the Vidyalankara Pirivena in 1946, explicitly called for *bhikkhus* to engage in politics in order to ensure the successful rise of a Sinhala Buddhist state in the wake of colonialism.

Although Senanayake is sometimes described as having been complacently out of touch with the gathering wave of popular religious nationalism that would soon overwhelm him, in fact he did not fail to be alarmed. He tried to have the Vidyalankara Declaration withdrawn, and he attacked the political *bhikkhus* on various fronts, suggesting, for instance, that they had been taken over by communists. J. R., who was minister of finance in Senanayake's government, was in the front line of this attack, and he accused the political *bhikkhus* of misrepresenting Buddhism and of promoting heretical ideas.[5]

Under the energetic socialist policies of the SLFP governments led by the Bandaranaikes (first, S. W. R. D. and then his widow, Sirimavo) Sri Lanka became the most state-governed economy in South Asia,[6] and in economic terms the cost to the country was high. Meanwhile, Tamil resentment in response to SLFP policies on language, religion and minority rights had hardened. This combination of increasingly debilitating economic problems and increasingly dangerous intercommunal tensions provided the UNP its main chance, and in 1977, the party, now led by J. R., achieved a decisive electoral victory.

J. R.'s campaign promised economic reform through the encouragement of free enterprise and the liberalizing of trade through the removal of price controls and the provision of incentives for innovation and production. Also, he aspired to a "righteous society" or *dharmistha*, wherein the *Sangha* would embody an ideal which government would take as its model in ruling the people. J. R. explains that the "Lord Buddha" not only had in mind "the creation of a righteous society," but also "for the first time in world history it is the United National Party that accepted" such an ideal "as its political principle."[7] But in J. R.'s view, *dharmistha* emphatically requires the abstention of *bhikkhus* from direct political action: "the Buddha advised members of the Buddhist Sangha not to take part in politics. No one can say, however that he exhorted politicians not to study or follow his teachings." J. R. concludes that "the study of Buddhism . . . . must profit those who take an active part in politics,"[8] but this is so only because politicians are to learn from the example set by *bhikkhus* whose vocation transcends the political sphere.

Interestingly, J. R. does not seek to downplay the role of the *Sangha* in society; rather, he elevates it. Thus, when he was elected prime minister, his first public address was delivered, as if in an act of deference, at the Temple of the Tooth, in Kandy, repository of the most revered relics of the Buddha and a site of major significance for the history of Buddhism in Sri Lanka. In his address, J. R. proclaims again that "the U.N.P. government aims at building a new society on the foundation of the principles of Buddha *Dhamma*. We have a duty to protect the Buddha *sasana* and to pledge that every possible action would be taken to develop it. At the same time we expect to help the cause of other religions equally."[9] The idealizing dimension of this statement is clear, but we might notice also how the plain declaration about "duty" and "pledge" is qualified in ways that make it less straightforward than we might at first think. For instance, what are we to make of the words "expect" and "equally"? Aren't they ambivalent, if only because what we "expect" might well be disappointed, and "equally" might mean equal to Buddhism, or equal to one another but subordinate to Buddhism? It is ever the way with J. R. to combine a disarming plain-spokenness with undercurrents suggesting some further, not quite clearly declared agenda. This combination of effects helps to explain why his enemies typically found him Machiavellian, whereas his supporters praised his clarity and openness. I will return to this aspect of J. R.'s discourse by and by.

When he was elected prime minister in 1977, J. R. set about making changes to counteract what he saw as the destructive policies of his predecessors. But the election had been accompanied by violent outbursts in several parts of the island, and the Tamil grievances that J. R. wanted to address had already hardened; yet J. R. remained optimistic that his new policies would improve the situation. As I have pointed out in chapter 3, these policies included a new constitution that shifted government away from a British parliamentary system to a Gaullist model centered on the office of president. A main argument for this far-reaching change was that a presidency would provide much-needed stability, thereby enabling reforms to be properly introduced and to take root. But J. R.'s enemies were quick to complain about his authoritarianism, and how he was casting himself as a quasi-monarch, modeled, as closely as he could manage in the circumstances, on the ancient Sinhala kings of the *Mahavamsa*. Indeed, as president, J. R. was not shy about describing himself as the 193rd head of state since the legendary founder Vijaya.[10]

Although the 1978 Constitution described Buddhism as Sri Lanka's "foremost religion" that the state should "protect and foster," J. R. resisted attempts to make Buddhism the official state religion, and he refused to meet with *bhikkhus* who wanted to argue against his position. Also, he changed the university admissions policy, which had discriminated against Tamils (though the problem remained complex), and he set up a plan for district development councils that would enable minority concerns to be better addressed.

In short, J. R.'s reforms aimed to counteract the more aggressively chauvinist policies of the SLFP, and it is easy to feel some influence of the liberal principles J. R. had learned from his mentor, D. S. Senanayake. Yet the *dharmistha* ideal, together with J. R.'s conception of himself as the living representative of a great lineage going back to the earliest part of *Mahavamsa* remind us that he was far from being a thoroughgoing secularist, and that Sinhala Buddhist interests remained close to his political heart.

The Accelerated Mahaweli Program[11] is a case in point. This government-supported irrigation project was designed to create hydroelectric power and to make the Dry Zone (to the north and east of the central highlands) habitable by large numbers of settlers. The project was to be a showcase for J. R.'s enterprising new economic policies, serving the common good. Yet J. R. also imagined the Accelerated Mahaweli Program as a continuation of the great irrigation achievements of precolonial Sri Lanka, and he expected that the glories of the ancient Buddhist kingdoms would be reborn in a modern context. Yet, to Tamils, it seemed that their traditional territories were being taken over, and official accounts stressing economic development for the good of all jostled uneasily with suspicions that the real plan was to extend Sinhala hegemony. Elsewhere on the cultural front, J. R.'s intentions to support Sinhala institutions were less ambivalent, not least because his government provided substantial funds for the restoration of Buddhist temples and monuments; also J. R. provided public money to bring the *Mahavamsa*[12] up to date (thereby including himself in it).

To his enemies, J. R. seemed duplicitous, playing incompatible goods against one another in order to promote Sinhala Buddhist interests while appearing to be friendly to Tamil concerns. To his admirers, he was an exceptionally skillful negotiator who dealt pragmatically with a discouragingly difficult situation. Yet, in the upshot, whether hero or villain, J. R. was unable to prevent intercommunal violence from escalating, and flare-ups in the Jaffna Peninsula in 1979 were sufficiently alarming that the government introduced a Prevention of Terrorism Act (modeled on the Northern Ireland PTA). Still, the situation worsened and, faced with a general election in 1982, J. R. resorted to tactics that even his defenders find hard to take. Instead of holding the election, J. R. held a referendum, appealing to the people to extend his government for a further six years. The gamble paid off, and J. R. then consolidated his already powerful position by requiring every UNP member of parliament to submit an undated letter of resignation. The idea was that an unruly MP could be removed from office with a minimum of fuss at J. R.'s discretion. All he had to do was date the letter.

The escalation of intercommunal strife culminated in the Colombo riots of 1983, sparked by the killing of thirteen Sinhala soldiers in Jaffna. A misguided government decision to bring the bodies back to Colombo led to angry protests among the crowds gathered for the occasion. Violence then spread rapidly through the city, and Tamils were targeted. The number of people killed in this "Black July" orgy of violence is disputed. The official government estimate at the time was 250, but more recent assessments have suggested numbers ranging up to 1,000 and more.[13] Tamil businesses and residences were systematically destroyed, and some rioters were in possession of voters' lists enabling them to identify Tamil households. Also, the predominantly Sinhala armed forces did not intervene, and were evidently in collusion with the anti-Tamil rioters.

Order was not restored for a week, and, for almost half of that time, J. R. maintained a stunned silence. When at last, after three days, he gave a radio and television address,[14] he stated that although the recent events were regrettable, they were also a response by Sinhalas to attempts to divide their country, and he would now see to it that all members of parliament would take an oath to uphold a unified Sri Lanka. Notoriously, he offered no word of comfort, support, or compassion for the Tamil victims. Instead, during the following days, his government proposed that the riots were fomented by the JVP—that is, by Marxist revolutionaries. Ordinary Sinhalas were thus, to some substantial degree, let off the hook, but no amount of glossing could conceal the fact that animosities between Sinhalas and Tamils had now developed into a full-blown modern ethnic conflict.

When, eventually, J. R. was forced to make an accommodation with India to stop the violence and prevent direct Indian intervention, he found himself between a rock and a hard place. On the one hand, the madness of violence, terror, and extreme cruelty had to end, and an invasion by Indian armed forces had to be prevented. On the other hand, J. R. faced stiff resistance from his Sinhala compatriots who were convinced that any deal with India would mark the beginning of the end of Sinhala national identity. Predictably, the *bhikkhus* by and large were opposed to the Indo-Sri Lankan Agreement of 1987, though as usual the *Sangha* did not speak univocally and J. R. was not without support from a broad range of sympathizers. Nonetheless, activist *bhikkhus* figured prominently in mass antigovernment protests and demonstrations.

In 1986, activist *bhikkhus* helped to form the Movement for Protecting the Motherland (Mavbima Surakime Vyaparaya, or MSV), a grouping of Buddhist lay organizations and *bhikkhus*. Some elements of the MSV then joined forces with the radical JVP, which in turn called explicitly for the death of J. R. and even issued posters and pamphlets with the injunction, "Kill J. R."[15] They almost succeeded in doing exactly this in 1987, by lobbing a hand grenade into a meeting where J. R. was in attendance. In response, J. R. launched a violent campaign against the JVP, brought to a grisly if effective conclusion by his successor, Ranasinge Premadasa. Meanwhile, the IPKF came to grief in the north, unable to contain the LTTE, which was unwilling to decommission. Ironically, the Indian army got drawn into armed conflict with the LTTE, and was forced rather ignominiously to withdraw from Sri Lanka in 1990.

When J. R. resigned the presidency in 1988, he was eighty-two years old, and had survived an impossibly complex and dangerous period in his country's history. His successor as president, Ranasinge Premadasa, who oversaw the withdrawal of the IPKF and hunted down JVP insurgents with ruthless efficiency, was himself assassinated in 1993, probably by the LTTE. And so Sri Lanka remained still in the tangles of an all-but intractable conflict. The basic problems remained much as they were when J. R. was in office and as they remain today: the rights of minorities (especially the Tamils) in relation to the majority Sinhalas; the devolution of authority to the northern and eastern provinces (and their possible merger); the language question and its relation to Sinhala Buddhist identity; the implications of Sri Lanka aspiring to become *Buddha Rajya* (Buddhist state).

I have provided this brief account of some main events of J. R.'s career, partly to fill out the brief account in chapter 3, but also as a way of getting to his writing and to suggest how difficult it is to assess the relationship between J. R.'s Buddhist convictions and his politics. At the conclusion of their exhaustive two-volume study, his biographers acknowledge how "ambiguous and contradictory" J. R.'s legacy is, and how "enigmatic"[16] he has remained to friends, foes, and biographers alike. Thus, his Sinhala cultural nationalism coexists uncomfortably with his attempts to strengthen the political power of the Tamil minority; his quasi-monarchist inclinations relate uneasily to his espousal of democratic principles; his repeated admiration for *ahimsa* (nonviolence) did not prevent him from using extreme physical force and promulgating repressive legislation; his deference to the *Sangha* did not cause him to relent in his strenuous insistence on keeping the *bhikkhus* out of politics; his promotion of equal economic opportunity within a free enterprise economy was considered not incompatible with large government expenditures for the restoration of Buddhist antiquities.

It is not difficult to find evidence of inconsistency and ambivalence in the biographies of many eminent people—that is partly why they are interesting, and, in the end, we are all to some degree opaque to one another. But in J. R.'s case, the ambivalence is unusually provocative, and how it was produced by (or in turn contributed to) the descent of Sri Lanka into one of the world's most dangerous conflict zones provokes further consideration, especially if the religious question is to be adequately addressed. And so I want now to consider a sample of J. R.'s writings to see what they can tell us about the complex interplay between religion and politics in his thinking, thereby perhaps enabling some better understanding of the "enigma," and how J. R.'s interpretation of Buddhism might relate to the tragic events of 1983 and their aftermath.

A SEPARATION OF POWERS:
ANALYSIS AND IMAGINATION

In the autobiographical preface to *Men and Memories*, J. R. describes how, as a young man, he was a "voracious reader," and he goes on to explain that he "preferred history, current affairs, biography and political science to pure literature."[17] J. R. offers no further reflection on this preference, but his relegation of "pure literature" to a subordinate position indicates something significant about his own practice as a writer. Typically, that is, J. R. is good with facts; he understands current affairs about which he offers coherent analyses; he is a clear thinker and he has an appreciative grasp of history. But imagination is not his strong suit, and he was insufficiently able to grasp how his subtle intellectual arguments did not dissuade people from their passionately held convictions, especially about cultural identity.

We recall how, after the riots of 1983, J. R. remained silent for days, and, when he did speak, his television and radio remarks lacked imaginative identification with the plight of the Tamils. Although J. R. had read extensively in the Pali Canon, the Buddha's understanding of people's irrational resentments and prejudices seems to have eluded him in much the same way as did a taste for "pure literature."

Thus, in dealing with the Buddha's instructions about right speech, J. R. points out that a disciple "cannot knowingly lie," not even "for any advantage whatsoever." Rather, the Buddha "wants man to speak such words as are gentle, soothing to the ear, courteous and dear."[18] Well, the Buddha himself was not always courteous and dear, gentle and soothing, and the sense in which the parables, similitudes, and verbal pratfalls of the Discourses are not exactly the straightforward truth does not occur to J. R. as he assesses what right speech might mean. Elsewhere, he notices that the Buddha does indeed teach "by conversation," but J. R. develops this point by way of only a brief comment about "appropriate phrases," and he concludes that the teachings in question "are as fresh and binding to-day as they were in the time of the Buddha."[19]

In the manner of these examples, J. R.'s reflections on the Pali Canon are consistently plain and succinct, even to a fault. This habit of mind is evident also in his political writings, in which he returns repeatedly to a small set of core ideas, clearly stated and lucid, even if uncertainly imagined in relation to the complexities of actual experience.

As Seneviratne[20] says, J. R. develops one side of Dharmapala's agenda by insisting on the compatibility of Buddhism with science, and by looking to science to help in the development of a modern Sri Lankan economy. But, as we see, unlike Dharmapala, J. R. did not welcome the idea that *bhikkhus* should be politically active, and he opposed the Vidyalankara Declaration. Still, J. R. and Dharmapala shared a similar view of science as having a special relationship with the Buddha's teachings, and, in describing this relationship, J. R. focuses on the idea that modern science (unlike nineteenth-century positivism) conceives of matter as energy, thereby dissolving a false dichotomy between subject and object. In an essay on "Buddhism and Science" he argues also that Western attempts to "separate science from religion"[21] are misguided; by contrast, "the teachings of the Buddha, the greatest of the Indian Sages, are in accordance with modern Science" (22), which shows that matter "as we see it and feel it, is an illusion." Basically, matter is "a certain kind of energy" of the same nature as the "nature of pure thought" (25). This is the conclusion at which the Buddha also arrived, and the West has much to learn from this Indian tradition of philosophical reflection (26).

J. R. goes on to repeat the idea that "matter is a form of energy" (29), and argues that the Buddha understood how knowledge is not confined to investigations of the external material world, but that the "searchlight" must be turned "inwards" (30) if we are to achieve a proper understanding of ourselves and of the universe. In "Buddhism and Marxism" J. R. repeats this argument, suggesting that (unlike Marxism) Buddhism is "in consonance with the most advanced teachings of modern science" (98), and that "mind and matter are only different manifestations of the same energy" (105). Consequently, "the Path then lies not in the outside world, but within ourselves" (100).

By proposing this special affinity between Buddhism and modern science, J. R. is able to argue that science is good for a Buddhist society such as Sri Lanka; yet he is also able to suggest that a merely instrumental or external application of science is limited. The Buddha teaches that truth and happiness are internal; consequently, the achievements of science in the external world will not make us happy. At best, science and technology are means to an end, enabling the material betterment of society in a way that will help people to pursue the real, inward happiness that the Buddha prescribes. Thus, "science will not find a permanent answer to man's search after happiness, though material comforts science may provide in increasing quantity and quality" (29–30). It follows that "the politician and the scientist should co-operate for the common good" (27) by alleviating "the problems of hunger and poverty" (28) and seeking to secure material well-being, always mindful that problems "arising from the greed and lust of men cannot be solved by Western scientific methods alone" (32).

Although these arguments appear straightforward, they are carefully considered and their implications are complex. For instance, the suggestion that modern science is consistent with Buddhism becomes, in J. R.'s hands, a way of *separating* the purest form of Buddhism from the material and social uses of scientific technology. That is, on the level of theory, J. R. effects a synthesis between science and Buddhism, enabling him to embrace science for the material betterment of a Sri Lankan Buddhist society. Yet he also argues that, for

practical purposes, science deals mainly with the external world and its appli-
cations are guided by politicians who are concerned about material welfare and
the common good. By contrast, the *bhikkhus* represent an ideal that should remind people of the limitations of the kinds of happiness provided by external
goods alone. As representatives of this ideal, the *bhikkhus* therefore should remain uncontaminated by politics as they explore the higher scientific truth that
matter is energy, beyond the separation of subject and object.

There is an elegant prestidigitation, here, as J. R. suggests that the theoretical synthesis of Buddhism and science entails a separation of powers
whereby the *bhikkhus* are kept out of the political domain. Thus, the *bhikkhus*
are to "lead morally perfect lives, perfect in thought, speech and action. Morally
perfect, they seek to realize spiritual perfection, which, according to the Buddhist ideal, is non-attachment" (8). Consequently, "Buddhism and Politics are
terms which refer to two different systems of human thought and activity," and
the Buddha himself is said to have advised members of the *Sangha* "not to take
part in politics" (33).

In his resistance to *bhikkhu* activism J. R. therefore parts company with his
mentor Dharmapala, but, ironically, he deploys another favorite Dharmapala
trope to help him to do so. That is, like Dharmapala, J. R. routinely criticizes
the *Sangha* for becoming caught up in ritualism and superstition, but J. R.'s aim
is not to get the *bhikkhus* to waken up to a political role; rather, he wants to free
them from distractions that would cause them to lose focus on the inner life.
Dharmapala's argument is therefore used to promote a result opposite to the
one sought by Dharmapala himself, even though the strenuous dismissal of ritualism, and the optimistic assertion that *nibbana* is attainable "here and now,"
without complex mediations and ritual observances, remains the same. "Fatal-
ism, ritual and ceremony," says J. R., are the result of "wrong beliefs," and the
"fatalists" and "reincartionists" who say "let us build temples and organize
pinkamas so that we may gain merit in future births" are merely causing "im-
measurable harm" (34–35). In a further essay, J. R. attacks devotees who turn
the Buddha into a "Myth," building dagobas and shrines and seeking help from
the gods through ritual observance. By contrast, the Buddha's teaching is simple: "Ye suffer from yourselves"—that is, no one other than ourselves can effect
our liberation: "no one can purify another" (38), and each of us alone must attend to the renunciation of self and cultivation of the inner life.

By reproving the *bhikkhus* for excessive indulgence in ritual, J. R. also
encourages their disengagement from festivities that, again, would bring Buddhism close to the political realm. But he not only wants the *bhikkhus* to remain
apart from politics; he insists that, in a certain sense, they remain apart from
one another. That is, each cultivates the inner life alone, and J. R. stresses the

importance of this irreducible individualism. Thus, for instance, he refuses to define Buddhism as a philosophy or a religion, and prefers to describe it as a "Path" that is different for each person: "It is also not correct to call his [the Buddha's] teaching a religion or a philosophy, though it contains the accepted truths of both. In the last analysis, it is a Path to a certain goal; a Way along which one must travel alone" (77). And so "the Buddha emphasizes the Way" (99), and the "Path then lies not in the outside world, but within ourselves" (100), and "the individual . . . must tread the Path alone" (96). Moreover, each step along the Path is to be perfect and cannot be taken for any ulterior motive: "I think the goal and the road are one. Every step must be as pure as the goal itself. There can be no impure steps to attain a pure goal. I say this because I know that violence brings hatred."[22] The link J. R. makes here between the purity of the Path (when truly followed) and nonviolence (*ahimsa*) is, again, a central principle of his thinking as a whole. Thus, he states that "Ahimsa (Non-Violence) is one of the cardinal principles of my life," going on to explain how formative Gandhi was in helping to bring him to this conviction.[23] Elsewhere, he commends the "*ahimsa* preached by the Buddha"[24] and promulgated by the Buddhist Emperor Asoka.

The three linked ideas that I have now briefly described remain at the heart of J. R.'s thinking. First, the *bhikkhus* are discouraged from engaging in politics and in superstitious observances; second, we are reminded that each human being walks the Path alone and each person's internal journey is different; third, the Path entails nonviolence. Clearly these positions represent an idealized view of what it means to be a *bhikkhu*, but, more important, they confirm a division of power between the *Sangha* and the political realm. By maintaining an elevated view of a *bhikkhu*'s true calling, J. R. shows himself to be a devout Buddhist, even as he contrives to ensure that the *bhikkhus* stay within their own special precinct. J. R. never hesitates about these matters, and he returns repeatedly to the same cluster of arguments about science, politics, the Path, *ahimsa*, and the vocation of the *bhikkhu*. Not surprisingly, his speeches and essays frequently give no hint of J. R.'s own Buddhist commitment; he was, after all, mainly a politician and preferred not to mix political issues with religion. Yet J. R. well knew also that his Buddhism was politically important, and if he were to succeed in politics, he would need to affirm and promote the value and integrity of Sinhala nationalism, especially in its resistance to colonial rule. But because he argued strenuously to separate the *Sangha* from politics, J. R. could not link the *bhikkhus* directly to the nationalist cause. Instead, he focused on other aspects of Sri Lanka's rich Buddhist heritage; however, in doing so, he failed sufficiently to imagine the dangers inherent in the cultural nationalism that he promoted for his own political purposes.

RELIGION, CULTURE,
AND THE "LAW OF THE JUNGLE"

As a quasi-monarchical president who saw himself part of a line going back to Vijaya and who admired the emperor Asoka, J. R. could be enthusiastically chauvinist when he felt the need. "We are engaged now in rebuilding a nation," he tells an audience, and "culture" is "an important part of that process."[25] To this end, he recommends developing "an art which, in the words of that Ancient Chronicle, *The Mahavamsa*, is 'one with the religion and the people'" (25), and in this context he frequently invokes the Dharmapalite idea of a Sinhala awakening. For instance, he talks about "a state of cultural coma" (28), and how "the people of Free Lanka have awakened after several centuries, and are seeking to express themselves according to their own traditions and genius" (25). During the late nineteenth century, as Buddhists in Sri Lanka "were awakening to an understanding of their rights," a cultural campaign followed "to preserve all that was characteristic of Sinhalese dress, customs and manners,"[26] and the example of the Indian independence struggle helped "to quicken the awakening consciousness of our people."[27] Predictably, this awakening is closely bound up with religion and language. Thus, J. R. argues that religion is "one of the chief factors"[28] in the shaping of culture, and he is clear about the foundational importance of Buddhism for this process in Sri Lanka:

> But from the beginning of the Buddhist civilization in Ceylon there is recorded history of the development of our culture, and what we call culture today in Ceylon sprang from that day. So owing to the influence of the great teaching of the Buddha, the ruins of Anuradhapura; the beautiful rock statues that exist there; the temples; the dagobas; and later in the Kandyan period the Kandyan dance forms are all results of the Buddhist civilization that prevailed in Ceylon.[29]

In short, Buddhism shaped Sri Lankan civilization from the beginning, and the continuity of this great and "unique" (30) legacy informs the postindependence awakening that J. R. heralds and promotes. Although he acknowledges that Sri Lankan "Buddhist culture" today must coexist with "other cultures," he emphasizes that Buddhist culture will remain "the most predominant" (31).

Sri Lanka's cultural distinctiveness is closely tied also to language, and in a speech to the State Council in 1944, J. R. proposes roundly that "language, Sir, is one of the most important characteristics of nationality"; moreover, "it is because of our language that the Sinhalese race has existed for 2,400 years."[30] In a further address in 1982, J. R. points out that modern Sinhalas are descendants of the "Vijayan clan," and have remained Buddhist through an "unbroken history" in which the "Sinhala language" is a central component.[31]

J. R.'s reference to the "Sinhalese race" alerts us, again, to how readily, during the Buddhist revival, cultural differences were racialized in discourse about Sri Lankan national identity. "There are racial characteristics that mould culture,"[32] J. R. assures us, going on to demonstrate the point by asserting that "racial characteristics have given the Germans a particular form of opera," and by assuring us that he could detect "racial characteristics" in a dance exhibition where the Sinhalas appeared as quite distinctive when compared to "the Mongolian and Polynesian races" (29). J. R. approves of the fact that Sinhala dance forms remain "pure and undefiled" (27), and he issues a warning against the mingling of cultures. "Racial characteristics," he says, are basic to the "unique contribution" of different groups, and what is "unique to Ceylon, national to Ceylon and patriotic" (31–32) must be preserved uncontaminated. J. R. concludes by rejecting any idea of "a synthesis of cultures" (32).

J. R.'s nonsense remarks about opera and dance confirm how uneasily his mind moved in matters having to do with the creative imagination in general. But more to the point is the clarity with which a racialized theory of identity, language, and religion emerges from his comments about Sinhala culture. In this context, a pressing question arises about how J. R.'s cultural nationalism relates to his insistence that, for practical purposes, religion and politics should be kept separate. Ever the astute analyst, J. R. does suggest a way of bridging the gap, at least in theory.

In a brief address at a *Buddha Jayanti* celebration, J. R. begins by reminding his audience of how "inextricably entwined" Sri Lanka's history is with the "Buddha Dhamma,"[33] and how the Buddha himself chose Sri Lanka "for the preservation of his teaching" (96). Thus, the land is full of dagobas, and "in no other part of the world are so many relics of the Buddha enshrined." Yet J. R. ends by offering a reminder: "The Buddha and his Dhamma can only act as guides to the individual who must tread the Path alone" (96). This return of the argument from the cultural domain to the private is, as we have seen, characteristic. The *bhikkhus* are called upon to live an exemplary life devoted to the inner Path, but just as with politics, so also the products of culture are burdened by material encumbrances and attachments from which the *bhikkhus* are free. At best, religious artifacts therefore might help to guide people toward the Path, and, in this view, culture promotes an ideal, in the pursuit of which the artifacts are themselves jettisoned. Also, because this pursuit is experienced by individuals in irreducible, particular ways, and is internal and nonviolent, it follows that culture, truly understood, cannot become the instrument of communal factionalism.

For their part, many *bhikkhus* distrusted J. R.'s brand of Buddhism, not only because it was aimed at keeping them out of politics, but also because it was too much an intellectual construct.[34] And indeed, for example, J. R.'s cherished *dharmistha* remained pretty much in a Platonic realm while, in actuality,

Sri Lanka burned. Also, as we see, J. R. insisted on the separation from the political sphere of the exemplary, inner-Path *bhikkhus*; yet, he deployed the rhetoric of Sinhala Buddhist nationalism for transparently political purposes when he needed to, partly to help promote an economic agenda, but also to secure Sinhala hegemony. By mixing religion and politics in this way, J. R. ended up doing what he did not want the *bhikkhus* to do, and his analytical elegance fails to conceal this uncomfortable fact. Consequently, even as he preached *ahimsa* and *dharmistha*, J. R. fanned the flames of ethnic conflict by promoting a Sinhala cultural nationalism defined by religion. Yet, as his response to the 1983 riots shows, he failed to imagine how he had helped to foment the situation that genuinely horrified him.

In a telling moment, J. R. confides to readers that "it was my destiny to steer Sri Lanka through one of the traumatic periods of its history during the eighties," when "the island-nation was torn by violence and ethnic strife."[35] Interestingly, J. R. talks here of violence and ethnic strife as if they had nothing directly to do with him, the steersman appointed by destiny to guide his nation through the storm. We might feel that some further imaginative understanding could have allowed J. R. further insight into his own involvement in seeding the storm in the first place, and, indeed, of continuing to be part of the turbulence. But J. R. could not easily imagine the process of regressive inversion in which he was so painfully involved, and how religious idealism could become detached from *ahimsa*, and how ethnic resentment and anger could be infused with an unbounded religious passion.

Certainly, J. R. knew that people who were usually nonviolent might, in particular circumstances, behave in violent ways, and he witnessed enough mob violence, terrorism, and state repression to understand the human proclivity for irrational and destructive behavior. Yet he also believed that "the human species developed from beast to man and then to civilised man," and in this process "the law of the jungle was replaced by law and order."[36] On this model, violence is a return to the law of the jungle, a merely regressive behavior. There is some truth in that view, but it neglects the significant further fact that violence in modern ethnic conflict zones marked by religion is invested with a highly dangerous religious intensity. Consequently, enemies can be demonized in the name of a higher principle, regardless of the fact that the higher principle itself condemns such demonizing, as well as the violence that follows from it. Regression indeed occurs, but it does not simply abandon the higher ideals and return to "the law of the jungle"; rather, it injects a religious passion for the absolute into the violent process itself.

Those among the *bhikkhus* who saw J. R. as too much an intellectual were not far wrong. Still, there is no reason to believe that he was merely Machiavellian, or that he was insincere about the values he espoused. But what should J. R.

have done? Clearly, it would have been better had he seen the limitations of his own Sinhala Buddhist cultural nationalism and pursued, instead, some more secular, pluralist, multiethnic political vision. But in that case, he probably would not have been successful politically, given the terms of the debate when he contested the elections against the SLFP. Yet it is not helpful to assume, either, that the riots, reprisals, mass murder, and dispossession were unavoidable. It is impossible to say what might have happened had different choices been made, different understandings brought to bear, and the modest conclusion here is, simply, that in assessing the lived complexities of religion in society, an educated imagination is an asset, as the Discourses of the Pali Canon especially teach us. One way to assess this claim is to consider the ill consequences that follow from its absence, as J. R.'s distinguished but tragically flawed career can show.

CHAPTER 7

CONCLUSION

In the preceding chapters I have focused on three Sinhala Buddhist writers who were highly influential in the Buddhist reform movement leading up to independence and, subsequently, in the shaping of a postcolonial Sri Lanka. A substantial amount of the work of these writers is available in English; consequently, the complexities of the debates in which they are involved can be assessed directly by a readership beyond Sinhala-speaking Sri Lanka.[1] This accessibility might in turn be helpful for readers interested in the global phenomenon of violent ethnic conflict, of which Sri Lanka offers such a compelling and important example.

My selection of authors does not represent the full range of Sinhala Buddhist opinion, which is varied, complex, and controversial in ways I cannot undertake to describe effectively. Nor do I deal with the Tamil political agenda (which is mainly secessionist rather than politico-religious) except insofar as it pertains to my examination of certain crucially influential interpretations of Buddhism that exemplify the process I describe as regressive inversion. To clarify what I mean by regressive inversion, I begin by offering some discussion of Buddhism, especially the Discourses of the Pali Canon.

In describing the emergence of Buddhism from its Vedic background, I have sought to clarify something of the profound coimplication of the Vedas and the Buddha's teaching. But I have wanted also to explore certain connections between an emergent Buddhist universalism and the Vedic experience of a world suffused with divine significance and sustained by the theory and ritual of sacrifice. I explore these connections partly by way of a distinction between disjunctive and conjunctive language. That is, Buddhism thematizes the discontinuity between language and its referents; rigorous attention to the seductions and deceptions of language is thus a means of encouraging nonattachment. Yet the discipline and critical vigilance required by a thoroughgoing application of the principle of discontinuity can rapidly induce an excessive, scarcely humane austerity. And so there is a parallel between the extreme application of disjunctive language and the extreme, world-denying asceticism that the Buddha recommends avoiding. Yet we need also to avoid the uncritical assumption that language is mainly conjunctive and that we are able by the power of words to grasp the divinely ordered nature of things. In such a view, language is magical and, therefore, vulnerable to superstitious interpretations and manipulation by ritual experts, authoritarian priesthoods, and the like. If, on the one hand, excessive austerity is to be avoided, so also, on the other hand, is uncritical indulgence. Consequently, as we see, the Buddha's preaching about extraordinary nonattachment did not prevent his own ordinary engagement with the lives of his many interlocutors, and the Buddha's compassion is expressed through an interplay between a cool conceptual austerity and a warmly imaginative participation in the day-to-day concerns of a wide variety of people.

With this dialogical model in mind, I have considered how the Discourses draw attention to their own language, and how narrative indirection, timing, tone of voice, irony, satire, burlesque, parable, humor, and dramatized confrontation are deployed as pedagogical devices. Conceptual formulation of the Buddha's core doctrines cannot alone be expected to effect a profound change in people's self-understanding. Rather, the individual's affective life, including enculturated feeling-structures, tacit loyalties and prejudices, need to be engaged if the transformative power of the new teaching is to be experienced in ways that really make a difference. And so I am suggesting a broad correlation between conjunctive language and the processes of early nurture by means of which a sense of belonging is acquired, boundaries established, and feeling-structures cultivated. Largely unselfconscious, participatory experiences of such a kind precede the development of disjunctive reflection, by means of which the independently thinking adult emerges as an individual, autonomous moral agent.

Primordial ties to kin-groups, cultural institutions, and the like remain important because they provide stability for a developing human ego; however, such ties also readily impart an exclusionary sense of identity that can be a source of prejudice. The Buddha's universalizing vision directly challenges this kind of prejudice even while acknowledging the formative and humanizing influence of the enculturation process. Yet, as the Discourses show, it is treacherously easy—despite repeated warnings and caveats—for the Buddha's teachings about absolute freedom to be re-deployed, by a fatal misprision, to supercharge the primordial passions informing the exclusionary sense of identity entailed by group membership. This process is *regressive* insofar as it reaffirms prejudice based on exclusion (the very thing that the universal religious vision was designed to transcend). Also, it entails an *inversion* of value insofar as it draws power and conviction from the languages and vision of transcendence.

To show something of how the process of regressive inversion operates, I have considered the writings of three influential Sinhala Buddhists: Anagarika

Dharmapala (who spearheaded the Buddhist revival prior to independence), Walpola Rahula (who wrote during the independence struggle), and J. R. Jayewardene (president during the worst violence in the postindependence period). In each case, my argument depends on analyses of primary texts, and the cogency of the points I make is best judged by considering these analyses directly. Therefore, I will not attempt to redact my arguments in detail, except to notice that in these three writers, Buddhism is annexed to a cultural nationalism in which theories about race, language, and religion combine to describe a Sinhala identity empowered by a sense of special destiny. Thus, for Dharmapala, a golden-age utopianism combines with a passionate, universalizing religious vision to create the idea of a Sinhala civilization newly awakened and empowered by modern science. Rahula tells us that "the nation and the religion have to move together," and his lucid, ecumenical understanding of what the Buddha taught is uncomfortably contradicted by the militant "religionationalism" he admired—not least in the warlike epic hero, Dutthagamini. By contrast, Gamini Salgado's engaging autobiographical memoir evokes a lived, everyday "traditional" Buddhism that can help put in perspective Rahula's ideological polemic. J. R. Jayewardene's position on Buddhism remains a mixture of clarity and ambivalence as he attempts to combine a passionate resistance to *bhikkhu* activism with a cultural Buddhism that he knows to be politically useful. J. R.'s idealized *dharmistha* and the horrifying actuality of Black July mark the poles of a tragic contradiction with which he struggled but was unable to resolve.

My main interest in discussing these writers is to explore how seductive is the process whereby the liberating vision of a great religion is re-deployed to confirm prejudices that the religion itself expressly offers to transcend. Yet it is important also to notice that the Buddhist revival in modern Sri Lanka is not so much a recovery of the Buddha's teachings in the Pali Canon as an adaptation of Buddhism to specifically modern conditions. Andreas Wimmer[2] argues persuasively that, in general, modern ethnic conflicts are not revivals of ancient disputes, though they are often described as if they were; rather, they are products of modernity itself. That is, when modern democracies give power to the people, replacing traditional "sacred, inclusive hierarchies" (87) (such as monarchies), the identity of "the people" becomes a pressing issue. This is so because legitimacy depends on decisions about "which 'people' the state should belong to," and in such a context "the meaning of ethnic distinctions changes radically" (91). Wimmer goes on to point out that the emergence of new modern nationstates frequently occurs before a strong civil society is able to develop (113), and, in situations where resources are scarce, the majority group becomes the beneficiary of political favoritism. Politics then are "quickly transformed into an arena of ethno-nationalist competition" (113).

Wimmer's analysis can help us to see more clearly how the Buddhist revival in Sri Lanka is not so much about the recovery of an ideal past as it is a means of asserting the modern preeminence of the Sinhalas as a "people." Yet by and large the revivalists did think of themselves as recovering a pristine Buddhism, and in the confusion of a high idealism espousing universal principles on the one hand, and a passionate vindication of ethnonationalist identity on the other, the seeds of the coming storm were sown. Certainly, the degree to which the writings of my three main authors (all of them pious Buddhists) were shaped by modernity becomes clear when we consider how they interpret the ancient Buddhist chronicle tradition.

As we have seen, the *Mahavamsa* is a court document addressing relationships between the monarchy and the *Sangha*. The identity of the "people" is not a main issue, and assorted, loosely affiliated groups constituting the population at large are not described or assessed in terms of distinct ethnic identities in a modern sense.

But in defining the Sinhalas by race, language, and religion, and as a people whose history and destiny legitimize their claim to preeminence, influential modern commentators have reread the ancient chronicle by way of a specific ethnonationalist agenda. In the process, the Buddha's universalism and the complex, compassionate discernment at the heart of his message are fatally annexed to the passionate intensities of ethnic competitiveness. The consequences have been (and continue to be) distressing in the extreme, but the tragic course of events in Sri Lanka is not atypical. Rather, the conflict is one among a number of similar violent ethnonationalist disputes that occurred globally during the second half of the twentieth century, the causes and unfolding of which are in many ways analogous.

Still, a final caution might remind us not to generalize with undue haste. None of us, after all, is ever quite as we are defined, and we remain to some degree opaque to ourselves and to one another. Something escapes, and that absence, or opaqueness, is our best, real opportunity for meeting the other; it lies also at the heart of what is meant by the dialogical. The Buddha himself taught us how we might proceed along such lines by way of a skillful interplay between principled understanding and personal encounter, and to the extent that we might be interested in containing ourselves from the worst things that we do to one another in the name of our highest ideals, his advice remains, still, to be heard.

NOTES

CHAPTER 1

1. The *Milindapanha*, a highly regarded postcanonical Pali text. The monk Nagasena answers questions posed by King Milinda. These include a discussion about words and their referents. Nagasena uses the example of a chariot to show that a chariot is an aggregate of parts and not a substantial unity. See *Milindapanha*, trans. T. W. Rhys Davids, *The Questions of King Milinda*, 2 vols. (Oxford: Oxford University Press, 1890), I, 41–45.

2. *The Vision of God*, ch. III, trans. Emma Gurney Salter (London: J. M. Dent, 1928), p. 71.

3. *Tao Te Ching*, 1, trans. D. C. Lau (Harmondsworth: Penguin, 1963), p. 57.

4. To some observers, Buddhism has seemed to be philosophical rather than religious. I deal with this distinction more fully in chapter 2.

5. I use the Pali spelling, Siddhattha Gotama, rather than the Sanskrit, Siddhartha Gautama. Because of my focus on the Pali Canon and on Sri Lanka, I will continue to use Pali terms where appropriate. I will deal with the Pali Canon in more detail in chapter 2.

6. This debate about semiotics has been central to literary theory during the past twenty-five or so years. The terms "conjunctive" and "disjunctive" are used by Thomas M. Greene, *Poetry, Signs, and Magic* (Newark: University of Delaware Press, 2005), to describe the basic opposition between what we might call the participatory and deconstructionist positions. Greene's terms are clear and nontechnical, and I will continue to use them as the argument develops.

7. An excellent summary of the debate is provided by Klaus K. Klostermaier, *Hinduism. A Short History* (Oxford: Oneworld, 2000), pp. 34 ff.

8. Dominic Goodall, ed., *Hindu Scriptures* (Berkeley: University of California Press, 1996), p. x, argues that the narrow use of the term is incorrect. The following account draws broadly on Goodall, and on the following: Harold Coward, *Scripture in the World Religions* (Oxford: Oneworld, 2000); Raimundo Panikkar, ed., *The Vedic Experience. Mantramanji. An Anthology of the Vedas for Modern Man and Contemporary Celebration* (Berkeley: University of California Press, 1977); Klaus K. Klostermaier, *Hinduism. A Short History* (Oxford: Oneworld, 2000); R. S. Misra, *Philosophical Foundations of Hinduism. The Vedas, the Upanishads and the Bhagavadgita: A Reinterpretation and Critical Appraisal* (New Delhi: Munshiram Manoharlal, 2002).

9. See Harold Coward, *Scripture in the World Religions*, pp. 105 ff.; Richard F. Gombrich, *Theravada Buddhism. A Social History from Ancient Benares to Modern Colombo* (London: Routledge, 2001; first published 1988), pp. 33 ff.

10. R. S. Misra, *Philosophical Foundations of Hinduism*, pp. 31–32, reviews the question, pointing out that "at certain places we find mention of the three Vedas and at some other places four Vedas are clearly specified"; nonetheless, "Vedic tradition regards the Vedas as four and not three."

11. *The Hymns of the Rgveda*, trans. Ralph T. H. Griffith, ed. J. L. Shastri (Delhi: Motilal Banarsidass, 1973; reprinted 1995), I, 164, 35.

12. *The Hymns of the Rgveda*, VIII, 44, 16; X, 7, 1; X, 186, 2.

13. *The Hymns of the Rgveda*, X, 90, 2, 6, 11–14.

14. Excluding epithets and possible indirect references, Prajapati is named at IX, 5, 9; X, 84, 43; X, 121, 10; X, 169, 4; X, 184, 1.

15. See, for instance, *Satapatha Brahmana*, XI, 1, 8, 2–4. Cited in Panikkar, *The Vedic Experience*, p. 385.

16. II, 3, 1, 5 (Panikkar, *The Vedic Experience*, p. 361).

17. II, 3, 1, 13 (Panikkar, *The Vedic Experience*, p. 363).

18. Steven Collins, *Selfless Persons. Imagery and Thought in Theravada Buddhism* (Cambridge: Cambridge University Press, 1982), p. 60, points to "a frequent idea of the *Brahmanas*: The sacrificer, in performing the ritual, makes the sacrifice his own self—*atman*; that is, he creates himself anew by birth into the ritual *loka*, and in doing so perpetuates his life, both here and hereafter."

19. *Satapatha Brahmana*, XIX, 2, 1, 1: "Of a truth man is born three times over in the following way. First, he is born from his mother and father. He is born a second time while performing the sacrifice that becomes his share. He is born a third time when he dies and they place him on the pyre and he proceeds

to a new existence. Therefore they say: 'Man is born three times'." (Cited in Panikkar, *The Vedic Experience*, pp. 393–94).

20. *Satapatha Brahmana*, XI, 2, 6, 13. Cited in Panikkar, *The Vedic Experience*, p. 394. See also Collins, *Selfless Persons*, p. 48.

21. See Collins, *Selfless Persons*, pp. 48–49: "just as after a sojourn in a ritually sacred *loka* the sacrificer returns to human society, so after a second lifetime in a *loka* after death, it is imagined that there is a return to earth, to the world of human society."

22. *Satapatha Brahmana*, III, 6, 2, 26. Cited in Panikkar, *The Vedic Experience*, p. 387.

23. *Satapatha Brahmana*, XI, 5, 6, 1–3. Cited in Panikkar, *The Vedic Experience*, p. 394.

24. *Satapatha Brahmana*, XI, 2, 6, 13. Cited in Panikkar, *The Vedic Experience*, p. 402.

25. See Panikkar, *The Vedic Experience*, p. 419: "Brahman, in the first Vedic period, means prayer and even sacrifice; in the Upanisadic period it means absolute Being and Ground, precisely because the sacrifice was considered to be such a Ground." See also Collins, *Selfless Persons*, p. 60: "At the same time, the sacrifice is said to be the same as *brahman*; that is, the efficacy of sacrificial power rests on the power which supports the whole universe." Dominic Goodall, *Hindu Scriptures* (Berkeley: University of California Press, 1996), p. xvii, points out that "brahman shifts in meaning so that it becomes identified with the origin of the universe."

26. *Maitri Upanisad*, IV, 6, trans. Valerie J. Roebuck (London: Penguin, 2003), p. 361. Further references are cited in the text.

27. For concise accounts of *Samkhya*, see Klostermaier, *Hinduism*, pp. 242 ff.; K. M. Sen, *Hinduism* (Harmondsworth: Penguin, 1961; reprinted 1991), pp. 80 ff.; Karen Armstrong, *Buddha. A Penguin Life* (New York: Penguin, 2001), pp. 44 ff.

28. Sen, *Hinduism*, p. 8.

CHAPTER 2

1. I use the Pali spelling, Siddhattha Gotama, rather than the Sanskrit Siddhartha Gautama. I will continue to use Pali terms, because of my focus on the Pali Canon and on Sri Lanka.

2. There are many studies on the life of the Buddha. Michael Carrithers, *The Buddha* (Oxford: Oxford University Press, 1983) and Karen Armstrong, *Buddha. A Penguin Life* (New York: Penguin, 2001) are two well-known examples. For a survey of the topic, see D. E. Shaner, "Biographies of the Buddha," *Philosophy East and West*, 37: 3 (1987), 303–22.

3. Because of its nontheism and emphasis on rationality, Buddhism has seemed to some commentators to be philosophical rather than religious. Yet the quest for absolute liberation, the idea of collecting and storing merit, the organized monastic life and ritual, might well be regarded as religious. The opposition between philosophy and religion is itself misleading, and is partly a consequence of Western secularism. Richard F. Gombrich, *Theravada Buddhism. A Social History from Ancient Benares to Modern Colombo* (London and New York: Routledge, 1988; reprinted 2001), p. 3, points out that Theravada Buddhists refer to Buddhism as the *Sasana*, or Teaching, rather than religion or philosophy. See also Klaus K. Klostermaier, *Buddhism. A Short Introduction* (Oxford: Oneworld, 1999), pp. 202–5, "Buddhism as Philosophy and Religion", and Walpola Rahula, *What the Buddha Taught* (Oxford: Oneworld, 2003, first published 1959), p. 5: "Is Buddhism a religion or a philosophy? It does not matter what you call it. Buddhism remains what it is whatever label you may put on it."

4. In the following notes, I will refer to the *Digha Nikaya* (Long Discourses) as DN; the *Majjima Nikaya* (Middle Length Discourses) as MN; and the *Samyutta Nikaya* (Connected Discourses) as SN. I will cite the standard *Sutta* numbers, followed by the English translation of the title, and page numbers for the English translation of cited material. The island simile occurs in *Mahaparinibbana Sutta*, DN 16 (2.26), trans. Maurice Walshe, *The Long Discourses of the Buddha. A Translation of the Digha Nikaya* (Boston: Wisdom Publications, 1995), "The Great Passing. The Buddha's Last Days," p. 245. The Buddha repeats this injunction elsewhere. See, for instance, *Cakkavati-Sihananda Sutta*, DN 26 (1), *Long Discourses*, "The Lion's Roar on the Turning of the Wheel," p. 395.

5. I use the term "Discourse" rather than "*Sutta*." As Walshe points out, "'discourse' is a makeshift rendering" of *Sutta*, which literally means "thread." Typically, a *Sutta* is "set within a slight narrative framework and always introduced by the words 'Thus I have heard', having supposedly been thus recited by the Ven. Ananda at the First Council." See *Long Discourses*, p. 533, note 2.

6. The Pali word *kusala* ("skillful") indicates the discerning cultivation of *kammically* profitable states of mind and disposition. The opposite of *kusala* is *akusala*. The term is not used to describe the rhetorical skill of the Discourses

as I have been assessing it, but such an application would be in keeping with the spirit of the Buddha's teachings. See Gombrich, *Theravada Buddhism*, p. 62.

7. Ernst Bloch, *The Principle of Hope*, trans. Neville Plaice, Stephen Plaice, and Paul Knight (Cambridge: MIT Press, 1995; first published 1959), Vol. 3, p. 1254.

8. For these examples (in addition to the *Mahaparinibbana Sutta*), see the *Bhayabherava Sutta*, MN 4 (3), "Fear and Dread," *The Middle Length Discourses of the Buddha. A New Translation of the Majjhima Nikaya*, trans. Bhikkhu Nanamoli, edited and revised by Bhikkhu Bodhi (Boston: Wisdom Publications, 1995), p. 102; *Ariyapariyesana Sutta*, MN 26 (13), "The Noble Search," *Middle Length Discourses*, p. 256; *Mahasaccaka Sutta*, MN 36 (20 ff.), "Greater Discourse to Saccaka," *Middle Length Discourses*, p. 337. The *Mahavagga* also recounts events that occurred directly after the Buddha's enlightenment. See *The Connected Discourses of the Buddha. A Translation of the Samyutta Nikaya*, trans. Bikkhu Bodhi (Boston: Wisdom Publications, 2000), pp. 1461 ff.

9. See *Culasaccaka Sutta*, MN 35, "The Shorter Discourse to Saccaka," and *Mahasaccaka Sutta*, MN 36, "The Greater Discourse to Saccaka," Middle Length Discourses, pp. 322 ff., 332 ff.

10. For a useful summary with a selection of texts, see Edward Conze, *Buddhist Scriptures* (London: Penguin, 1959), chapter 1, "The Buddha's Previous Lives," pp. 19 ff.

11. See. L. S. Cousins, "The Dating of the Historical Buddha: A Review Article," *Journal of the Royal Asiatic Society*, 6 (1996), pp. 57–63. Walshe concludes that, despite the lack of consensus, "Perhaps 'ca. 480–400' would be a reasonable guess," *Long Discourses*, p. 532. Klostermaier concurs: "Most Western scholars prefer dates of c. 480–400 B.C.E.," *Buddhism. A Short Introduction*, p. 27.

12. See Walshe, *Long Discourses*, pp. 47–48.

13. Modern historical scholarship casts doubts on various claims made in traditional accounts of the early Buddhist councils. See E. Lamotte, *History of Indian Buddhism from the Origins to the Saka Era* (Louvain: Institut Orientaliste, 1988). The following brief summary offers only a broad outline of a traditional understanding of how the Canon was assembled. It seems unlikely that five hundred *arahants* could recite the whole *Vinaya Pitaka* and *Sutta Pitaka* by the time of the first rainy season after the Buddha's death, but exactly how the teachings were collected and transmitted remains unclear.

14. The *Ariyapariyesana Sutta*, MN 26 (20), "The Noble Search," *Middle Length Discourses*, p. 261, has Brahma say: "There are beings with little dust in

their eyes who are wasting through not hearing the Dhamma," and "out of compassion" the Buddha agrees to teach his doctrine.

15. The Four Noble Truths are expounded frequently throughout the Discourses. See, for instance, *Samaditthi Sutta*, MN 9 (13–19), "Right View," *Middle Length Discourses*, pp. 134–45; *Saccavibhanga Sutta*, MN 141 (2 ff.), "The Exposition of the Truths," *Middle Length Discourses*, pp. 1097 ff.

16. See Walpola Rahula, *What the Buddha Taught*, p. 17: "it also includes deeper ideas such as 'imperfection', 'impermanence', 'emptiness', 'insubstantiality'." The wheel out of kilter is pointed out by Steve Hagen, *Buddhism Plain and Simple* (New York: Broadway Books, 1997), p. 25.

17. *Asankhatasamyutta*, SN 43 (I, 11), "Connected Discourses on the Unconditioned," *The Connected Discourses of the Buddha. A Translation of the Samyutta Nikaya*, trans. Bhikkhu Bodhi (Boston: Wisdom Publications, 2000), p. 1374. As Walpola Rahula says, "Nirvana is not the result of anything. . . . There is a path leading to the realization of Nirvana. But Nirvana is not the result of this path." See *What the Buddha Taught*, p. 40.

18. *Salayatanasamyutta*, SN 35 (III, 28), "Connected Discourses on the Six Sense Bases," *Connected Discourses*, p. 1143. In the previous paragraph the Buddha explained: "Bhikkhus, all is burning. . . . Burning with what? Burning with the fire of lust, with the fire of hatred, with the fire of delusion."

19. See *Culamalunkya Sutta*, MN 63 (5), "The Shorter Discourse to Malunkyaputta," *Middle Length Discourses*, p. 534.

20. References to the Noble Eightfold Path occur frequently. For a detailed account, see the *Saccavibhanga Sutta*, MN 141 (23 ff.), "The Exposition of the Truths," *Middle Length Discourses*, pp. 1100 ff.; *Mahacattarisaka Sutta*, MN 117 (1 ff.), "The Great Forty," *Middle Length Discourses*, pp. 934 ff.; *Mahavagga*, SN, Part V, *Maggasamyutta*, I, 8, "Connected Discourses on the Path," *Connected Discourses*, p. 1528 ff.

21. See, for instance, *Alagaddupama*, MN 22 (42 ff.), "The Simile of the Snake," *Middle Length Discourses*, pp. 235–36; *Anapanasati Sutta*, MN 118 (10 ff.), "Mindfulness of Breathing," *Middle Length Discourses*, pp. 942–43; *Dakkhinavibhanga Sutta*, MN 142 (5), "The Exposition of Offerings," *Middle Length Discourses*, pp. 1103–4.

22. Thich Nhat Hanh, *Living Buddha, Living Christ* (New York: Riverhead Books, 1995), pp. 184–85.

23. *Mahatanhasankhya Sutta*, MN 38 (17), "The Greater Discourse on the Destruction of Craving," *Middle Length Discourses*, pp. 353–54.

24. See, for instance, *Tevijjavacchagotta Sutta*, MN 71 (7), "To Vacchagotta on the Threefold True Knowledge," *Middle Length Discourses*, p. 588.

25. The five aggregates, or *khandhas*, are mentioned frequently. See *Khandhasamyutta* SN 22 (82), "Connected Discourses on the Aggregates," *Connected Discourses*, pp. 924–25.

26. For a careful account of this complex question, see Steve Collins, *Selfless Persons. Imagery and Thought in Theravada Buddhism* (Cambridge: Cambridge University Press, 1982).

27. *Abyakatasmyutta*, SN 44 (10), "The Book of the Six Sense Bases," *Connected Discourses*, p. 1394.

28. *Aggivacchagotta Sutta*, MN 72 (15 and 18), "To Vacchagotta on Fire," *Middle Length Discourses*, pp. 592 and 593.

29. See Collins, *Selfless Persons*, pp. 71, 50.

30. Rahula, *What the Buddha Taught*, p. 34.

31. Collins, *Selfless Persons*, p. 212.

32. *Mahatanhasankhya Sutta*, MN 38 (3, 5, 26), "The Greater Discourse on the Destruction of Craving," *Middle Length Discourses*, pp. 349 ff. Page numbers are cited in the text.

33. Note 411 on p. 1232 explains that the "being to be reborn" is the *gandhabba*, but asks us not to imagine "someone (i.e., a disembodied spirit standing nearby watching the future parents having intercourse, but a being driven on by the mechanism of *kamma*, due to be reborn on that occasion)." Again, this caveat draws attention to the difficulty, as the editor's (disjunctive) explanation corrects the uncomfortable literalism, which is, however, not easy to avoid. How we are to think about the "being" that is "driven on" and "due to be reborn" remains unclear.

34. *Kandaraka Sutta*, MN 51, "To Kandaraka," *Middle Length Discourses*, pp. 443 ff. Page numbers are cited in the text.

35. *Culahatthipadopama Sutta*, MN 27, "The Shorter Discourse on the Simile of the Elephant's Footprint," *Middle Length Discourses*, pp. 269 ff.

36. *Bahuvendaniya Sutta*, MN 59, "Many Kinds of Feeling," *Middle Length Discourses*, pp. 502 ff. Page numbers are cited in the text.

37. *Pasadika Sutta*, DN 29 (1), "The Delightful Discourse," p. 427. Page numbers are cited in the text.

38. *Brahmajala Sutta*, DN 1 (8), "The Supreme Net. What the Teaching Is Not," *Long Discourses*, p. 69.

39. *Abhayarajakumara Sutta*, MN 58 (10), "To Prince Abhaya," *Middle Length Discourses*, p. 500.

40. *Mahaparinibbana Sutta*, DN 16 (2.26), "The Great Passing. The Buddha's Last Days," *Long Discourses*, p. 245.

41. *Pasadika Sutta*, DN 29 (29), "The Delightful Discourse," *Long Discourses*, p. 436.

42. *Mahaparinibbana Sutta*, DN 16, "The Great Passing. The Buddha's Last Days," *Long Discourses*, pp. 231 ff. Page numbers are cited in the text.

43. *Ambattha Sutta*, DN 3, "About Ambattha. Pride Humbled," *Long Discourses*, pp. 111 ff. Page numbers are cited in the text.

44. *Kevaddha Sutta*, DN 11, "About Kevaddha. What Brahma Didn't Know," *Long Discourses*, pp. 175 ff. Page numbers are cited in the text.

45. *Kakacupama Sutta*, MN 21, "The Simile of the Saw," *Middle Length Discourses*, pp. 217 ff. Page numbers are cited in the text.

46. *Mahasihanada Sutta*, DN 8, "The Great Lion's Roar," *Long Discourses*, pp. 151 ff.

47. *Mahasatipatthana Sutta*, DN 22 (10), "The Greater Discourse on the Foundations of Mindfulness," *Long Discourses*, p. 339.

48. *Mahadukkhakkhanda Sutta*, MN 13, "The Greater Discourse on the Mass of Suffering," *Middle Length Discourses*, pp. 179 ff. Page numbers are cited in the text.

49. *Lohicca Sutta*, DN 12, "About Lohicca. Good and Bad Teachers," *Long Discourses*, pp. 181 ff. Page numbers are cited in the text.

50. *Potthapada Sutta*, DN 9, "About Potthapada. States of Consciousness," *Long Discourses*, pp. 159 ff. Page numbers are cited in the text.

CHAPTER 3

1. See Steven Kemper, *The Presence of the Past. Chronicles, Politics and Culture in Sinhala Life* (Ithaca and London: Cornell University Press, 1991), p. 32, for these several meanings of the word.

2. For an account of the two chronicles, see Kemper, *The Presence of the Past*, pp. 34 ff.

3. For a succinct account of the myth and its context, see Rajiva Wijesinha, *Sri Lanka in Crisis 1977–88* (Colombo: Council for Liberal Democracy, 1991) pp. 1 ff. Kemper, *The Presence of the Past*, p. 55, discusses variants of the tale.

4. *The Mahavamsa or The Great Chronicle of Ceylon*, trans. Wilhelm Geiger, PhD, assisted by Mabel Haynes Bode, PhD (London: for the Pali Text Society by Henry Froude, Oxford University Press, 1912), chapter 25, p. 175. Dutthagamini's victory is described in chapter 25, and I will cite page numbers in the text.

5. Richard F. Gombrich, *Buddhist Precept and Practice. Traditional Buddhism in the Rural Highlands of Ceylon* (Delhi: Motilal Banarsidass, 2nd ed., 1991), p. 300.

6. Kemper, *Presence of the Past*, p. 105. See Alice Greenwald, "The Relic on the Spear: Historiography and the Saga of Dutthagamani," in *Religion and Legitimation of Power in Sri Lanka*, edited by Bardwell L. Smith (Chambersburg, PA: Anima Books, 1978), pp. 13–35, on the ancient chronicles and their "charter-like function," which is "specifically intended to establish and affirm Sinhalese religio-national consciousness," despite "ostensible discrepancies with orthodoxy" (30).

7. Kemper, *Presence of the Past*, p. 127.

8. Anuradhapura was attacked in 933 C.E. and annexed to the Chola empire.

9. See note 2, on naming the chronicles. The account of Parakramabahu I is found in *Culavamsa*, trans. Wilhelm Geiger, 2 vols. (Colombo: Ceylon Government Information Department, 1953), chapters 63–64.

10. *Mahavamsa*, trans. Geiger, page 4, note 4, says the meaning "is simply that the Yakkhas were driven back to the highlands (giri) in the interior, where they can still be found today."

11. David Little, *Sri Lanka. The Invention of Enmity* (Washington, DC: United States Institute of Peace Press, 1994), pp. 27–28. The case is slightly overstated, however, as Little draws a strong contrast between the two accounts. But there is some terror in the *Dipavamsa*, and some solicitude in the *Mahavamsa*.

12. *The Dipavamsa. An Ancient Buddhist Historical Record*, edited and translated by Hermann Oldenberg (London: Williams and Norgate, 1879), pp. 122–23.

13. Heinz Bechert, "The Beginnings of Buddhist Historiography: Mahavamsa and Political Thinking," ed. Bardwell Smith, *Religion and Legitimation of Power in Sri Lanka* (Chambersburg, PA: Anima Books, 1987), p. 7.

14. As Kemper says, *Presence of the Past*, p. 20: "there is historical evidence that some Sinhala caste communities of today—the Karava, Salagama, and Durava—were recognizable Indian groups that settled in Sri Lanka after the thirteenth century." See also Richard Gombrich and Gananath Obeyesekere, *Buddhism Transformed. Religious Change in Sri Lanka* (Princeton: Princeton University Press, 1988), p. 178.

15. Stanley Jeyaraja Tambiah, *Buddhism Betrayed? Religion, Politics and Violence in Sri Lanka* (Chicago: University of Chicago Press, 1992), p. 173; *Sri Lanka. Ethnic Fratricide and the Dismantling of Democracy* (Chicago: University of Chicago Press, 1991; first published 1986), p. 140.

16. See Tambiah, *Buddhism Betrayed*, pp. 134–35.

17. See Gombrich and Obeyesekere, *Buddhism Transformed*, p. 178; Kemper, *Presence of the Past*, p. 45.

18. See Neluka Silva, ed., *The Hybrid Island. Culture Crossings and the Invention of Identity in Sri Lanka* (London, New York: Zed Books, 2002).

19. *Buddhism Transformed*. Page numbers are cited in the text.

20. There are many excellent historical accounts of colonialism and the Buddhist revival, leading to independence. See especially K. M. De Silva, *A History of Sri Lanka* (London: C. Hurst, 1981); *Reaping the Whirlwind. Ethnic Conflict, Ethnic Politics in Sri Lanka* (New Delhi: Penguin, 1998). For a concise account, see Gombrich, *Buddhist Precept and Practice*, pp. 23–43; H. R. Perera, *Buddhism in Sri Lanka* (Kandy: Buddhist Publication Society, 1988), pp. 59 ff.

21. See Kitsiri Malalgoda, *Buddhism in Sinhalese Society 1750–1900* (Berkeley: University of California Press, 1976), pp. 33–34. Malalgoda's account of "The Impact of the Portuguese and Dutch Missionary Efforts," pp. 28–49, is especially informative.

22. Cited in K. M. De Silva, "Buddhist Revivalism, Nationalism, and Politics in Modern Sri Lanka," ed. James Warner Bjorkman, *Fundamentalism, Revivalists and Violence in South Asia* (Riverdale, MD: Riverdale Company, 1988), p. 111.

23. R. Spence Hardy, *The British Government and Idolatry in Ceylon* (London: Crofts and Blenkarn, 1841). Page numbers are cited in the text.

24. See Kitsiri Malalgoda, *Buddhism in Sinhalese Society 1750–1900*, p. 204: "The traditional religion of the Sinhalese appeared to the missionary as a massive evil structure that had to be destroyed before conversion proper could begin."

25. Gananath Obeyesekere, "Religious Symbolism and Political Change in Ceylon," *Modern Ceylon Studies*, 1: 43–68.

26. See Gombrich and Obeyesekere, *Buddhism Transformed*, pp. 207 ff. A remarkable collection of documents on this topic is provided by Tennakoon Vimalananda, *Buddhism in Ceylon Under the Christian Powers, and the Educational and Religious Policy of the British Government in Ceylon 1797–1832* (Colombo: M. D. Gunasena, 1963).

27. *Buddhism Transformed*, p. 208.

28. George D. Bond, *The Buddhist Revival in Sri Lanka. Religious Tradition, Reinterpretation and Response* (Delhi: Motilal Banarsidass, 1992), p. 18.

29. See H. L. Seneviratne, *The Work of Kings. The New Buddhism in Sri Lanka* (Chicago: University of Chicago Press, 1999), pp. 49–50.

30. *Buddhism Transformed*, p. 209.

31. See Littlle, *Sri Lanka. The Invention of Enmity*, p. 17.

32. See John Capper, *Buddhism and Christianity. Being an Oral Debate Held at Panadura* (Colombo: P. K. W. Siriwardhana, 1955), preface. The main arguments of the debate are transcribed from various reports.

33. See Gombrich and Obeyesekere, *Buddhism Transformed*, p. 203.

34. See Gombrich and Obeyesekere, *Buddhism Transformed*, p. 237: "The widespread practice of meditation by laity is the greatest single change to have come over Buddhism in Sri Lanka (and indeed in the other Theravadin countries) since the Second World War."

35. See Seneviratne, *The Work of Kings*, pp. 41 ff.

36. See Gombrich and Obeyesekere, *Buddhism Transformed*, pp. 212 ff.

37. Bond, *The Buddhist Revival*, provides a careful account of these complexities.

38. R. A. L. H. Gunawardena, "The People of the Lion: Sinhala Consciousness in History and Historiography," in *Ethnicity and Social Change in Sri Lanka* (Colombo: Navamaga Printers, 1985), p. 97. Gunawardena is cited by Tambiah, *Buddhism Betrayed*, p. 132, as part of a persuasive argument about the modern construction of race.

39. Tambiah, *Buddhism Betrayed*, p. 134. Page numbers are cited in the text.

40. S. J. Tambiah, *Sri Lanka. Ethnic Fratricide and the Dismantling of Democracy* (Chicago: University of Chicago Press, 1991; first published 1986), p. 7.

41. See Tambiah, *Buddhism Betrayed*, p. 131–2, especially note 5.

42. Darini Rajasingham-Senanayake, "Identity on the Borderline: Modernity, New Ethnicities, and the Unmaking of Multiculturalism in Sri Lanka," in Silva, *The Hybrid Island*, p. 55: "By the 1871 census the term 'race' appeared for the first time along with the category of nationality, with 78 'nationalities' and 24 'races' being recorded in Ceylon."

43. Kemper, *Presence of the Past*, p. 22.

44. *Dharma-Vijaya (Triumph of Righteousness) or the Revolt in the Temple* (Colombo: Sinha Publications, 1953). Page numbers are cited in the text.

45. The following account draws broadly on K. M. De Silva, *A History of Sri Lanka* and *Reaping the Whirlwind*; David Little, *Sri Lanka. The Invention of Enmity*; Rajiva Wijesina, *Sri Lanka in Crisis 1977–88*; K. N. J. Dharmadasa, *Language, Religion and Ethnic Assertiveness: The Growth of Sinhalese Nationalism in Sri Lanka* (Ann Arbor: University of Michigan Press, 1992); Jonathan Spencer, ed., *Sri Lanka: History and the Roots of Conflict* (London: Routledge, 1990); Nira Wikramasinghe, *Ethnic Politics in Colonial Sri Lanka 1927–47* (New Delhi: Vikas Publications, 1995).

46. De Silva, *Reaping the Whirlwind*, p. 128.

47. This controversial policy was named "Sinhala Only."

48. Rioting occurred in 1956, when a mob attacked a peaceful Tamil protest against the language policy. The 1958 riots, again focused on the language policy, were more violent, and were sparked by a protest organized by *bhikkhus*. See De Silva, *Reaping the Whirlwind*, pp. 122–23.

49. M. R. Narayan Swamy, *Tigers of Lanka* (Colombo: Vijitha Yapa Publications, 6th ed., 2005; first published 1994), p. 36.

50. This estimate is offered by Estanislao Oziewicz, *Globe and Mail*, 3 August 2006.

51. *The Statesman*, 1 July 2006, describes the LTTE as offering "a virtual admission of guilt," not least (presumably) because India's withdrawal of active support was a setback for the Sri Lankan Tamil cause, and the LTTE are concerned to encourage India's reinvolvement.

52. *Globe and Mail*, 3 August 2006.

53. See Chandra R. de Silva, "The Plurality of Buddhist Fundamentalism: An Inquiry into Views among Buddhist Monks in Sri Lanka," in *Buddhist Fundamentalism and Minority Identities*, edited by Tessa J. Bartholomeusz and

Chandra R. de Silva (Albany: State University of New York Press, 1998), pp. 53-73, on the diversity of opinion among *bhikkhus*.

CHAPTER 4

1. A concise account of Dharmapala's life and writings is provided by Ananda W. P. Guruge, *The Unforgettable Dharmapala* (Place of publication uncited: 1st Books, 2002). See also Gananath Obeysekere, "Personal Identity and Cultural Crisis: The Case of Anagarika Dharmapala of Sri Lanka," edited by Frank E. Reynolds and Donald Capps, *The Biographical Process: Studies in the History and Psychology of Religion* (The Hague: Mouton, 1976); and Bhikkhu Sangharakshita, *Anagarika Dharmapala: Biographical Sketch* (Kandy: Buddhist Publication Society, 1964). The following account draws on these sources.

2. Ananda Guruge, ed., *Return to Righteousness. A Collection of Speeches, Essays and Letters of the Anagarika Dharmapala* (Ceylon: Government Press, 1965); p. xlix prints the article. All further quotations are from this edition, and page numbers are cited in the text.

3. In a letter (15 June 1915), Dharmapala describes himself as "a Buddhist Missionary." See *Return to Righteousness*, p. 537.

4. Dharmapala provides an interesting memoir, with details of his early life and education, "Memories of an Interpreter of Buddhism to the Present-Day World," in *Return to Righteousness*, pp. 681 ff. He describes meeting Gunananda, who was a family friend, "nearly every day" (685).

5. See "Memories of an Interpreter," pp. 688–89, for Dharmapala's account of the iconoclastic Mahant ("head of the Hindu fakir establishment") who controlled the temple.

6. George D. Bond, *The Buddhist Revival in Sri Lanka: Religious Tradition, Reinterpretation and Response* (Delhi: Motilal Banarsidass, 1992), p. 60.

7. H. L Seneviratne, *The Work of Kings. The New Buddhism in Sri Lanka* (Chicago: University of Chicago Press, 1999), pp. 27, 28.

8. *Return to Righteousness*, p. XVIII.

9. Dharmapala uses these terms frequently; examples are provided in the following discussion.

10. Dharmapala refers to Buddhism as a religion (as distinct from a system of philosophy). See, for instance, "Buddhism Past and Present," *Return to Righteousness*, p. 486, on the "purely religious civilization" of the ancient Sinhala Buddhists.

11. Eva K. Neumaier, "Missed Opportunities. Buddhism and Ethnic Strife in Sri Lanka and Tibet," edited by Harold Coward and Gordon S. Smith, *Religion and Peacebuilding* (Albany: State University of New York Press, 2004), p. 75.

CHAPTER 5

1. Richard F. Gombrich, *Buddhist Precept and Practice. Traditional Buddhism in the Rural Highlands of Ceylon* (Delhi: Motilal Bandarsidass, 1991), pp. 47, 65.

2. *Buddhist Precept and Practice*, pp. 85–87.

3. Walpola Rahula, *The Heritage of the Bhikkhu*, trans. K. P. G. Wijaya-surendra (New York: Grove Press, 1974; first published 1946).

4. H. L. Seneviratne, *The Work of Kings. The New Buddhism in Sri Lanka* (Chicago: University of Chicago Press, 1999), p. 135. It should be noted also that the *bhikkhus* were not of one mind about the politicization issue, and, influential as Rahula was, the positions he espoused were opposed by counterarguments by *bhikkhus*, Buddhist lay organizations, and the press. See Urmila Phadnis, *Religion and Politics in Sri Lanka* (London: C. Holt, 1976), pp. 164 ff.

5. Gamini Salgado, *The True Paradise* (Manchester: Carcanet, 1977; first published 1993).

6. The following account draws mainly on the following: Udaya Malla-warachchi, "Walpola Rahula. A Brief Biographical Sketch," edited by Somaratna Balasooriya et al., *Buddhist Studies in Honour of Walpola Rahula* (London: Gordon Fraser, 1980), pp. vi ff.; E. F. C. Ludowyk, "Thinking of Rahula," in *Buddhist Studies in Honour of Walpola Rahula*, pp. 133 ff. A helpful brief account of Rahula's career, also drawing mainly on these sources, is provided by Stanley Jeyaraja Tambiah, *Buddhism Betrayed? Religion, Politics and Violence in Sri Lanka* (Chicago: University of Chicago Press, 1992), pp. 23–26.

7. Mallawarachchi, "Walpola Rahula," p. vii.

8. Ludowyk, "Thinking of Rahula," p. 138.

9. Ludowyk, "Thinking of Rahula," p. 138.

10. Walpola Rahula, *What the Buddha Taught* (Oxford: Oneworld, 2003; first published 1959). Pages numbers are cited in the text.

11. Walpola Rahula, *History of Buddhism in Ceylon. The Anuradhapura Period, 3rd Century BC–10th Century AC* (Colombo: M. D. Gunasena, 2nd ed., 1966; first published 1956). Page numbers are cited in the text.

12. Seneviratne, *The Work of Kings*, p. 191.

13. *History of Buddhism*, p. 77. See also p. 153.

14. In the following account, page numbers are cited in the text.

15. In the following account, page numbers are cited in the text.

CHAPTER 6

1. J. R. Jayewardene provides an informative autobiographical account in *Men and Memories. Autobiographical Recollections and Reflections* (New Delhi: Vikas Publishing House, 1992), preface, pp. v ff. The standard biography is K. M. De Silva and Howard Wriggins, *J. R. Jayewardene of Sri Lanka. A Political Biography*, Vols. 1 and 2 (Honolulu: University of Hawaii Press, 1988 and 1994). The following summary draws on these sources.

2. See David Little, *Sri Lanka. The Invention of Enmity* (Washington, DC: United States Institute of Peace Press, 1994), p. 148, note 45.

3. See James Manor, *The Expedient Utopian: Bandaranaike and Ceylon* (Cambridge: Cambridge University Press, 1984).

4. The Vidyalankara Declaration, which was passed on 13 February 1946, is published in Walpola Rahula, *The Heritage of the Bhikkhu*, translated by K. P. G. Wijayasurendra and revised by the author (New York: Grove Press, 1974), Appendix II, pp. 131–33.

5. See H. L. Seneviratne, *The Work of Kings. The New Buddhism in Sri Lanka* (Chicago: University of Chicago Press, 1999), p. 144. See also p. 203, note 22, on "an incident in 1947, in which Rahula and some others were assaulted by thugs, widely believed to be candidate (later Finance Minister, President) J. R. Jayewardene's, in election-related violence." Senanayake's alarm and concern to some degree provoked the *bhikkhus*. In a speech in 1946, he "expressed his distress that the monks should be thronging the galleries of the State Council," and thereby helped to goad the *bhikkhus* into making a hostile response. See Urmila Phadnis, *Religion and Politics in Sri Lanka* (London: C. Hurst, 1976), pp. 163–64.

6. De Silva and Wriggins, *J. R. Jayewardene*, II, 333, describe J. R.'s intention to reverse "the policies of the 1960s and 1970s, during which Sri Lanka had developed into the most state-dominated economy of South Asia. The model he sought to emulate was Singapore."

7. J. R. Jayewardene, *Buddhist Essays* (Sri Lanka: Department of Government, 4th ed., 1982; first published 1942), pp. 116–17.

8. Jayewardene, *Buddhist Essays*, p. 33.

9. Cited in Steven Kemper, *The Presence of the Past. Chronicles, Politics and Culture in Sinhala Life* (Ithaca: Cornell University Press, 1991), p. 174.

10. See Kemper, *Presence of the Past*, p. 171: "His enemies frequently pointed out that there was also something unmistakable about the monarchist imagery of Jayewardene's administration"; and p. 170: "on a state visit to Washington in 1984 he introduced himself to President Reagan as Sri Lanka's 193rd head of state, tracing himself back to Vijaya." Rajiva Wijesinha, *Sri Lanka in Crisis 1977–88. J.R. Jayewardene and the Erosion of Democracy* (Colombo: Council for Liberal Democracy, 1991), preface, pp. v–viii, links J. R.'s personal quest for power to the erosion of democracy. Yet, as de Silva points out, "The new constitution, in fact, is by far the most notable and resolute initiative in ethnic reconciliation taken in the recent political history of the island." See K. M. De Silva, *Managing Ethnic Tensions in Multi-Ethnic Societies. Sri Lanka 1880–1985* (Lanham, MD: University Press of America, 1986), p. 303. For a concise appraisal of J. R.'s self-serving interests in formulating the new constitution, see V. P. Vittachi, *Sri Lanka—What Went Wrong* (New Delhi: Navrang, 1995), pp. 80–83.

11. The controversy about government intentions remains unsettled, and in the following brief summary I describe the main opposed points of view. See De Silva and Wriggins, *J. R. Jayewardene*, I, 14; Kemper, *Presence of the Past*, pp. 128–29; Patrick Peebles, "Colonization and Ethnic Conflict in the Dry Zone of Sri Lanka," *Journal of Asian Studies* 49 (1990), 30–55.

12. See Kemper, *Presence of the Past*, pp. 175 ff.

13. De Silva and Wriggins, *J. R. Jayewardene*, II, 561, suggest "between 500 and 600"; speech by President Chandrika Kumaratunga at the 21st Anniversary of "Black July," Presidential Secretariat, Colombo, July 23, 2004, mentions the (incomplete) findings of a Truth Commission appointed in 2001: "They have been able to find evidence of nearly a 1000 [sic] killings during that period." For a disturbing reflection on the violence, see Jonathan Spencer, "Popular Perceptions of the Violence: A Provincial View," edited by James Manor, *Sri Lanka in Change and Crisis* (London: Croom Helm, 1984), pp. 187–95. Spencer discusses the mood of ordinary Sinhalas and the wave of "popular panic" (190) and "paranoid fantasies" (191) about Tamils that had been building before 1983.

14. The following summary draws on Wijesinha, *Sri Lanka in Crisis*, pp. 76–77.

15. See De Silva and Wriggins, *J. R. Jayewardene*, II, 646.

16. De Silva and Wriggins, *J. R. Jayewardene*, II, 714, 722.

17. *Men and Memories*, p. vi.

18. *Buddhist Essays*, "The Ethics of the Buddha," p. 3.

19. *Buddhist Essays*, "Three Sermons of the Buddha," pp. 62, 67.

20. Seneviratne, *The Work of Kings*, pp. 139 ff.

21. *Buddhist Essays*, p. 21. Further page numbers are cited in the text.

22. *Men and Memories*, p. 123.

23. *Men and Memories*, pp. 159 ff.

24. *Buddhist Essays*, p. 109.

25. *Selected Speeches. 1944–1973* (Colombo: H. W. Cave, 1974), "The School of Music and Dancing," p. 25. Further page numbers are cited in the text.

26. *Men and Memories*, p. 6.

27. *Men and Memories*, p. 32.

28. *Selected Speeches*, p. 28.

29. *Selected Speeches*, p. 29.

30. *Selected Speeches*, p. 7.

31. *Buddhist Essays*, pp. 114–15.

32. *Selected Speeches*, p. 29. Further page numbers are cited in the text.

33. *Buddhist Essays*, p. 95. Further page numbers are cited in the text.

34. See Little, *Sri Lanka*, p. 93.

35. *Men and Memories*, p. xii.

36. *Men and Memories*, p. 178.

CHAPTER 7

1. The position of the English language in modern Sri Lanka has been controversial. J. R. Jayewardene looked to English as "the link language" with the best potential for enabling a fruitful discourse among "peoples of the world" (*Men and Memories*, p. 176). J. R.'s inclination to idealize shows through in this piously optimistic statement, but the notion persists that English is an effective means

of opening up Sri Lanka for discussion internationally. Also, English is especially useful as a means of making available the benefits of modern science and technology. In 2005, Dayan Jayatilleke in an interview with Bruce Matthews makes a similar point to J. R.'s: "Jayatilleke further avers that Lanka is in danger of fostering a triple isolationism (island, religion, language) and of failing to see that its multiculturalism is in fact a 'bridge' to the rest of the world." Cited from Bruce Matthews, "Christian Evangelical Conversions and the Politics of Sri Lanka," transcript of a presentation at York University, Toronto, 31 May 2006, p. 12.

2. Andreas Wimmer, *Nationalist Exclusion and Ethnic Conflict: Shadows of Modernity* (Cambridge: Cambridge University Press, 2002). Page numbers are cited in the text.

SUGGESTIONS FOR
FURTHER READING

PART I READING BUDDHISM

Armstrong, Karen, *Buddha. A Penguin Life*. New York: Penguin, 2001.

Bechert, H. (ed). *The Dating of the Historical Buddha*. Gottingen: Vandenhock and Ruprecht, 1991.

Beyer, S. *The Buddhist Experience: Sources and Interpretation*. Belmont, CA: Dickenson, 1974.

Bloomfield, M. *The Religion of the Veda*. New York: G.P. Putnam's, 1908.

Carrithers, Michael. *The Buddha*. Oxford: Oxford University Press, 1983.

Chakravarti, S. C. *The Philosophy of the Upanishads*. Calcutta: University of Calcutta Press, 1935.

Collins, Steven. *Selfless Persons. Imagery and Thought in Theravada Buddhism*. Cambridge: Cambridge University Press, 1982.

Coward, Harold. *Scripture in the World Religions*. Oxford: Oneworld, 2000.

Frauwallner, E. *History of Indian Philosophy*, V. M. Bedekar, trans., 2 vols. Delhi: Motilal Banarsidass, 1983–1984.

Gethin, R. *The Foundations of Buddhism*. Oxford: Oxford University Press, 1998.

Gombrich, Richard F. *Theravada Buddhism. A Social History from Ancient Benares Modern Colombo*. London: Routledge, 2001.

Goodall, Dominic (ed.). *Hindu Scriptures*. Berkeley: University of California Press, 1996.

Harvey, P. *An Introduction to Buddhism: Teachings, History and Practice.* London: Cambridge University Press, 1990.

Hawkins, B. K. *Buddhism.* Upper Saddle River: Prentice-Hall, 1999.

Hopkins, T. J. *The Hindu Religious Tradition.* Belmont: Dickenson, 1971.

Ions, V. *Indian Mythology.* London: Paul Hamlyn, 1967.

Kenoyer, J. M. *Ancient Cities of the Indus Valley Civilization.* Karachi: Oxford University Press, 1998.

Keown, Damian, *A Dictionary of Buddhism.* Oxford: Oxford University Press, 2004.

Klostermaier, Klaus K. *Hinduism. A Short History.* Oxford: Oneworld, 2000.

———. *Buddhism. A Short History.* Oxford: Oneworld, 1999.

Ling, T. *The Buddha: Buddhist Civilization in India and Ceylon.* London: Temple Smith, 1973.

Lopez, D. S. *Curators of the Buddha: The Study of Buddhism under Colonialism.* Chicago: University of Chicago Press, 1995.

Mahadevan, T. M. P. *Outline of Hinduism.* Bombay: Cetana, 1960.

Malalasekera, G. P. (ed.). *Encyclopaedia of Buddhism.* Colombo: Government of Sri Lanka, 1961–.

Misra, R. S. *Philosophical Foundations of Hinduism. The Vedas, the Upanishads and the Bhagavadgita. A Reinterpretation and Critical Appraisasl.* New Delhi: Munshiram Manoharlal, 2002.

Murti, T. R. V. *The Central Philosophy of Buddhism.* London: George Allen and Unwin, 1955.

Norman, K. R. *Pali Literature, Including the Canonical Literature in Prakrit and Sanskrit of all the Hinayana Schools of Buddhism.* Wiesbaden: Harrassowitz, 1983.

Panikkar, Raimundo (ed.). *The Vedic Experience. Mantramanji. An Anthology of the Vedas for Modern Man and Contemporary Celebration.* Berkeley: University of California Press, 1977.

Prothero, S. *The White Buddhist: The Asian Odyssey of Henry Steel Olcott.* Bloomington: Indiana University Press, 1996.

Rahula, Walpola. *What the Buddha Taught.* Oxford: Oneworld, 2003.

Rajaram, N. S., and D. Frawley. *Vedic Aryans and the Origins of Civilization*. New Delhi: Voice of India, 1997.

Staal, J. F. *Agni. The Vedic Ritual of the Fire Altar*, 2 vols. Berkeley: University of California Press, 1983.

Talageri, S. G. *The Aryan Invasion Theory and Indian Nationalism*. New Delhi: Voice of India, 1993.

Walker, B. *The Hindu World: An Encyclopedic Survey of Hinduism*. 2 vols. New York: Praeger, 1968.

PART II READING SRI LANKA

Balasooriya, Somaratna et al. *Buddhist Studies in Honour of Walpola Rahula*. London: Gordon Fraser, 1980.

Bartholomeusz, Tessa J., and Chandra R. De Silva (eds.). *Buddhist Fundamentalism and Minority Identities*. Albany: State University of New York Press, 1998.

Bhikkhu Sangharakshita. *Anagarika Dharmapala: Biographical Sketch*. Kandy: Buddhist Publication Society, 1964.

Bjorkman, James Warner (ed.). *Fundamentalism, Revivalists and Violence in South Asia*. Riverdale, MD: Riverdale Company, 1988.

Bond, George D. *The Buddhist Revival in Sri Lanka. Religious Tradition, Reinterpretation and Response*. Delhi: Motilal Banarsidass, 1992.

Capper, John. *Buddhism and Christianity. Being an Oral Debate Held at Panadura*. Colombo: P. K. W. Siriwardhana, 1955.

De Silva, K. M. *Reaping the Whirlwind. Ethnic Conflict, Ethnic Politics in Sri Lanka*. New Delhi: Penguin, 1998.

———. *Managing Ethnic Tensions in Multi-Ethnic Societies*. Sri Lanka 1880–1985. Lanham, MD: University Press of America, 1986.

———. *A History of Sri Lanka*. London: C. Hurst, 1981.

De Silva, K. M., and Howard Wriggins, *J.R. Jayewardene of Sri Lanka. A Political Biography*. 2 vols. Honolulu: University of Hawaii Press, 1988 and 1994.

Dharmadasa, K. N. J. *Language, Religion and Ethnic Assertiveness: The Growth of Sinhalese Nationalism in Sri Lanka*. Ann Arbor: University of Michigan Press, 1992.

Gombrich, Richard F. *Buddhist Precept and Practice. Traditional Buddhism in the Rural Highlands of Ceylon.* Delhi: Motilal Banarsidass, 1991.

Gombrich, Richard F., and Gananath Obeyesekere. *Buddhism Transformed. Religious Change in Sri Lanka.* Princeton: Princeton University Press, 1988.

Gooneratne, Yasmine. *Relative Merits: A Personal Memoir of the Bandaranaike Family of Sri Lanka.* London: C. Hurst, 1986.

Guruge, Ananda W. P. *The Unforgettable Dharmapala.* Place of publication uncited: 1st Books, 2002.

Guruge, Ananda W. P. (ed.). *Return to Righteousness. A Collection of Speeches, Essays and Letters of the Anagarika Dharmapala.* Ceylon: Government Press, 1965.

Jayewardene, J. R. *Men and Memoirs. Autobiographical Recollections and Reflections.* New Delhi: Vikas Publishing House, 1992.

———. *Buddhist Essays.* Sri Lanka: Department of Government, 4th ed., 1982.

———. *Selected Speeches* 1944–1973. Colombo: H. W. Cave, 1974.

Kapferer, Bruce. *Legends of People, Myths of State: Violence, Intolerance, and Political Culture in Sri Lanka and Australia.* Washington, DC: Smithsonian Institution Press, 1988.

———. *A Celebration of Demons.* Bloomington: Indiana University Press, 1983.

Kemper, Steven. *The Presence of the Past. Chronicles, Politics and Culture in Sinhala Life.* Ithaca and London: Cornell University Press, 1991.

Little, David. *Sri Lanka. The Invention of Enmity.* Washington, DC: United States Institute of Peace Press, 1994.

Malalgoda, Kitsiri. *Buddhism in Sinhalese Society 1750–1900: A Study of Religious Revival and Change.* Berkeley: University of California Press, 1976.

Manor, James. *The Expedient Utopian: Bandaranaike and Ceylon.* Cambridge: Cambridge University Press, 1984.

Manor, James (ed.). *Sri Lanka in Change and Crisis.* London: Croom Helm, 1984.

Phadnis, Urmila. *Religion and Politics in Sri Lanka.* London: C. Holt, 1976.

Rahula, Walpola. *The Heritage of the Bhikkhu.* New York: Grove Press, 1974.

Salgado, Gamini. *The True Paradise.* Manchester: Carcanet, 1977.

Seneviratne, H. L. *The Work of Kings. The New Buddhism in Sri Lanka*. Chicago: University of Chicago Press, 1999.

Silva, Neluka (ed.). *The Hybrid Island. Culture Crossings and the Invention of Identity in Sri Lanka*. London: Zed Books, 2002.

Smith, Bardwell L. (ed.). *Religion and Legitimation of Power in Sri Lanka*. Chambersburg, PA: Anima Books, 1978.

Spencer, Jonathan (ed.). *Sri Lanka: History and the Roots of Conflict*. London: Routledge, 1990.

Swamy, M. R. Narayan. *Tigers of Lanka*. Colombo: Vijitha Yapa Publications, 6th ed., 2005.

Tambiah, Stanley Jeyaraja. *Buddhism Betrayed? Religion, Politics and Violence in Sri Lanka*. Chicago: University of Chicago Press, 1992.

———. *Sri Lanka. Ethnic Fratricide and the Dismantling of Democracy*. Chicago: University of Chicago Press, 1991.

———. *World Conqueror and World Renouncer*. Cambridge: Cambridge University Press, 1976.

Vimalananda, Tennakoon. *Buddhism in Ceylon Under the Christian Powers, and the Educational and Religious Policy of the British Government in Ceylon 1797–1832*. Colombo: M. D. Gunasena, 1963.

Vittachi, V. P. *Sri Lanka—What Went Wrong*. New Delhi: Navrang, 1995.

Wijesinha, Rajiva. *Sri Lanka in Crisis 1977–88. J. R. Jayewardene and the Erosion of Democracy*. Colombo: Council for Liberal Democracy, 1991.

Wikramasinghe, Nira. *Ethnic Politics in Colonial Sri Lanka 1927–47*. New Delhi: Vikas Publications, 1955.

Wilson, A. Jeyaratnam. *The Break-up of Sri Lanka: The Sinhalese-Tamil Conflict*. Honolulu: University of Hawaii Press, 1988.

Wimmer, Andreas. *Nationalist Exclusion and Ethnic Conflict: Shadows of Modernity*. Cambridge: Cambridge University Press, 2002.

INDEX